CW00566979

Praise for Breatl Communicat

Gentle and powerful, wry and straightforward, astute and appealing, Fiona Brennan-Scott takes the reader on a delightfully practical journey to become a Breathtaking Communicator. A true gem to read for those of us who realise that the art of great communication is the basis of everything.

Dr Lynda Shaw
Behavioural Neuroscientist,
Business Relationships Mentor, Speaker

"The ability to deliver clear, confident and concise speech is often regarded as a rare gift. However, few great speakers are born that way. They learn their craft, often without realising how. In this unique book, Fiona looks deep into the techniques that speakers use, both physical and emotional, and breaks them down into easily understood elements. Understanding your voice, and the way in which it works, is essential for anyone who uses oral communication - and that's pretty much everyone. I've never seen a book that offers such a comprehensive guide to the mechanics of speaking, and guides the reader to improve every aspect of their oral communication. It will become an invaluable tome for anyone who wants to be listened to."

Alan Stevens
Past President, Global Speakers Federation.

Fiona Brennan Scott has given us a classic new book, *Breathtaking Communication,* offering the reader pages of practical, guided advice, amazing tools and action oriented body and mind exercises to practice, all explained in easy to follow detail. Fiona's vast experience, passion and enthusiasm for the spoken word shines through on every page. It is a huge book, with each chapter offering enormous value and important information. Jump in and use the chapters as you like, as guided markers in your speaker journey, This content rich book is a must read for all speakers, experienced or new to the speaking world. Grab a copy today and revolutionize your speaking no matter where you are in your speaking career.

Renèe Lee Rosenberg
Career Management Coach, Anti-Ageism Advocate, Author, Speaker

---

Fiona Brennan-Scott's book gives very clear guidance to the source and anatomy of voice work. It is an ideal platform from which to start the journey into the discovery of our voices.

Professor Patsy Rodenburg O.B.E.
Patsy Rodenburg Associates

Breathtaking Communication

Tools and Techniques for Everyday Leaders

Fiona Brennan-Scott

ISBN: 978-1-7392166-0-3

Layout and Publishing support Divine Flow Publishing, UK

Cover Design Mark Wójcicki, Studio Stanley

Figures and illustrations by Alex Scott

Contents

Dedication

To those who have taught and inspired me,
though no book bears their names:
Mary Cummins
Joan Lee
Barbara Gillman
Alec

Foreword

Whether you are a professional speaker, with years of experience and hundreds of speeches under your belt, or starting out just realising the importance of the spoken word to your life and career, this book is for you. It will take you from where you are through your next few steps of development, regardless of your starting point.

Just like Fiona, whether in front or behind the curtains, the stage has always held an appeal for me. But the place I enjoy the most is standing in the backstage wings, as near to the technical crew as possible, as the last minute preparations for the opening scene are underway. There's a hushed freneticism about those moments: final checks, warm ups, last minute changes, nervous anticipation. The hard preparation work has been done - now comes the moment of truth.

That's what this book is about: the hard work before the moment of truth. But with each page, you'll pick up Fiona's passion and enthusiasm for doing the preparation work before the delivery that needs to be done. In fact, like her and me, you might begin to discover that all of the planning, practising and preparation that goes into giving a powerful presentation (or interview or performance) is every bit as fun and rewarding as the event itself.

Standing in the wings, waiting for your turn to take the stage - whether literally or metaphorically - is a magic moment to experience if you know you've done the preparation and are ready for action. You'll find the most comprehensive set of preparation tools in the pages of this book - more than enough to ensure you're ready for whatever stage awaits you.

Fiona suggests that the book can be accessed like a Treasury, using the chapter titles to decide where to dip in and extract valuable insights. I agree that this is what the book will become for you, but you'd be ill-advised to skip any of the chapters or appendices, in my opinion. There are nuggets of gold in every single chapter.

As someone who has been speaking for a living for three decades, each chapter gave me something to consider, something new to try and fresh insights into a world I know very well. The Resonator Scale definitely turned heads in our house, as I took up my speaker's pose in front of a mirror and loudly went through this vocal exercise, much to the amusement of my unsuspecting family. For those just starting out as speakers, this is more than a Treasury - it's a map, a guidebook and an instruction manual. And it goes way beyond the mere mechanics of speaking, incorporating many additional tips and tools, from interview technique to the structure of a good wedding speech.

But be warned: this is not a book you can just read. It's packed with practical exercises and advice that clearly comes from Fiona's own decades of experience. Reading the book is obviously a good start (a 'very good place to start'), but the real value will come from finding the time and space to practice what you read, and implement what you learn in these pages. And then, of course, to do them again and again - in private practice and public performance.

With this book as your guide, you're just going to get better and better at delivering the spoken word to an audience. And as far as I am concerned, that will make the world a better place.

Graeme Codrington

Speaker, Author, Expert on the Future of Work

CEO of TomorrowToday Global

Recipient of multiple speaking awards, including Speaker Hall of Fame recognition from the Professional Speakers Associations of the UK & Ireland, and of South Africa, and TEDx Shorts Global Featured Speaker 2021.

Introduction

Breathtaking communication is about audience engagement. As much goes on behind the scenes before this happens, I would like to take you 'backstage' to my own story before we begin proper!

These next few pages can be considered the setting of the stage. The curtains open in Chapter 1. If you're interested in knowing why I believe this book needs to be written, and why I believe I might be the right person to write it, read on. The unique combination of life experiences, studies and work we've each had come together to provide what we offer to any audience. Here are mine.

My audience experience

One of my earliest memories is of trips to the theatre. We were dressed up and bundled into the car, infused with my mother's perfume, applied minutes before, and we drove to Clonmel's White Memorial Theatre. Our car was parked in a side street and my mother's high heels echoed off the walls of the terraced townhouses as we rushed not to be late – a perennial problem for us if I remember correctly. My hometown, Clonmel, is a large town nestled in a valley and that grew around the river in Tipperary, south-east Ireland.

We joined other patrons climbing the stone steps of what used to be a Wesleyan chapel, I later discovered, and this explained the black wrought-iron gates to an ancient cemetery to the right of the building. There was much laughter, excitement and greetings. My parents were well-known in the town and avid supporters of the arts. Generous patrons made it possible for St. Mary's Choral Society to put on two musicals a year and garner many national AIMS[1] awards for the quality of their productions.

We were ushered to our seats, always the middle towards the back of the stalls, considered by Dad to be the best seats in the house.

Then, for me at least, the magic began. I had entered a wondrous place with red velvet, tightly packed seats, that you had to stay sitting on to keep them from popping closed – no mean feat when you're about three or four! The excitement was palpable and the giant, closed red velvet curtains held a secret waiting to be told. Added to this was the random sounds of the orchestra tuning up; the space was filled with promise and potential. It didn't sound like anything coherent could come together from such blows and screeches, but you knew from experience, it would.

The lights went down, and silence descended. A spotlight shone as the handsome Danny Carroll, musical director and conductor, appeared in his evening suit. The theatre exploded into applause as he took his place on the podium, bowed, turned, tapped his stand and lifted his baton. The overture played and as it ended to enthusiastic applause, a silence fell as the curtains parted.

The show had begun, and the world had faded far away.

I believe this was the appeal that resurfaced for me again and again – the power of engagement to transport people to a different place. I would be 15 when that would become a lifeline to me.

The theatre was a mainstay of our entertainment diet as a family. Four shows a year – two in Clonmel and two in Carrick-on-Suir, 13 miles away. I had a deep desire to be part of this world, especially when I saw child actors in a production of *Oliver!* But it wasn't easy for my parents, who ran four businesses and raised three daughters, to make the level of commitment required for rehearsals – this, I appreciated only later. Weekly ballet lessons or piano lessons were far more manageable, especially as we reached an age where we could take ourselves.

So, my expertise developed as a member of the audience.

Other performances included attending the Banna Cluain Meala's (Clonmel Marching Band) annual concert and viewing their marching on the High School field from the upstairs window of our house. They produced a powerful sound and were led by the same prolific musical director and band leader, Danny Carroll. He was also my mother's hairdresser during the week and that of many other ladies for whom a weekly hairdo was part of the respite from being a housewife. I'm sure the conversations around music (my mother was an accomplished pianist) and theatre saved a fortune on what would be spent on therapy these days!

I now recognise that my 'audience experience' was also informed by my experience of being raised in the Irish Roman Catholic Church. Mass – the Catholic term for a church gathering, provided a weekly performance and ritual which contributed to shaping me as an audience and sometimes participant. These finely dressed men on highly decorated stages, moved from pulpit to altar, and audience engagement was sprinkled throughout. We participated sometimes, but only as requested and only in monotone responses. We were lowly; they were elevated. The choir sung from lofty heights behind us. When I was nine or ten, my sister and I joined St Peter and Paul's Church Choir. That was wonderful. As I emerged into my teens, the focus moved from the challenge of singing in parts, to dressing up for the catwalk that was the journey to communion after the congregation had received, accompanied by our singing. This was the outlet for performance for me at this life stage!

I was in awe of the religious ritual and then one day it didn't make sense anymore. It coincided with the same year my father died, and I started drama lessons.

It's important to recognise that we all start out as audience. Our skills are developed and honed – when to listen, when to participate, when to respond and how to do that. We are unlikely to know the skills and techniques that are being used by the performers onstage, but we know two things: what works, and what doesn't. Even if we don't like something a performer is saying, singing, doing or playing, we can appreciate when it's good, when it touches us, and when it elicits a response.

That is what I've studied and learned to understand over the years, through being taught, through study and 22 years of teaching and coaching and training experience. That is what I want to pass on to others who engage with people – in meetings, interviews and on the business stage whether on or offline. It's as simple and as complicated as this:

> *How to engage with an audience and connect with them so that it works - so that you elicit a desired response.*

Being a drama student

In 1984, when I was 15, I had the opportunity to attend the first drama school in our town. The teacher was Mary Cummins, director of a musical every year since the White Memorial Theatre opened. She acted in others, and possibly in some that she directed too. She also sang in the choir of St. Mary's, a parish church in Clonmel. She was, and still is, a local legend.

For three years I trekked to the far side of the town to join other teenagers for one hour of drama classes. I remember the improvisations, playing with ideas, bouncing them off each other, the laughter and the feedback. It was magical. In pretending to be someone else, we developed as ourselves. It was a kind and safe place to do so; in the gable end of Mary's house, we were The Gable School Theatre. The best kind of business meeting has all those elements too, as we step into our professional roles.

For this reason, I believe every parent should encourage their child to do drama. Recently, I listened to a podcast where Andrew Scott (of *Sherlock's* Moriarty and *Fleabag's* Hot Priest fame[2]) described how he was sent to drama classes because he had a stammer. Having seen him on screen as well as onstage (Noel Coward's *Present Laughter)*, drama classes have clearly led to him becoming a nuanced and accomplished actor. But there are many thousands of people around you in life who never aspired to an acting career, who would attribute a lot of their life skills development and confidence to drama lessons. In studying pedagogy as part of my Trinity College London qualification, I would go on to learn that play is an essential form of learning. If we can extend play into adulthood, we are giving ourselves enormous opportunities to learn. This is why you will find exercises and games interspersed throughout this book; some no doubt taught to me by Mary.

The sudden death of my father when I was 14, along with my mother's grief, resulted in drama being a great escape. Additionally, my two sisters and I were teenagers, and along with the inevitable challenges and confusion of that age, needed to work through suffering the additional grief and loss. Imagine how great a relief it was to pretend to be someone else for an hour a week. The inner workings of our mind can benefit enormously for an outlet in effective spoken communication in some form.[3]

Engaging an audience and being engaged by a speaker is a unique gift to humankind. We see engagement in nature between animals, but the additional power of knowledge and words adds the potential to transform the human experience. Why would you not want to learn how to do that, and do it well?

Fast forward a couple of years and I applied to read Drama at Trinity College Dublin. Despite being called for a coveted interview, I failed to secure a place. I realised in the interviews that I knew precious little about drama, except prancing around the stage and all the preparation that went into that as an actor. My second choice was to attend Business School and I accepted a place to study Marketing and Administration at the Dublin Institute of Technology. Before long, over a pint of Guinness in the local pub, two lads invited me to co-found a Drama Society. We won a national drama competition in our second year, and it is still running to this day. The drama coach who came in weekly to work with us was a furious little Scotsman called Alec and he was brilliant, writing and directing the winning play based on the life of Rudolf Nureyev. I know nothing else about Alec, I can't even recall his surname, but some of the exercises here will have been inspired by him.

By 1990 I was living in South Africa, having gone with a rucksack for four months and stayed for thirteen years. Looking back, I recognise that drama never quite left me. As soon as I became involved in church again at 23, I was asked to do sketches as points of contact in services. The most hilarious results were often when I needed a second person and roped in my fiancé to help me. I also used drama as a way of understanding a message when helping as a Sunday school teacher and youth leader. I had no experience of either but, having held a Bible in my hands for the first time that year, I realised it was a brilliant collection of stories. It was a great source document for scripts.

This rolled along for several years as I slowly built up a career in the corporate world, firstly in administration and then in international marketing. I loved my final role in corporate work and believe I was good at my job. But when our first baby came along, I was burning the candle at both ends. When my husband asked what would make me happy, out of seemingly nowhere, I announced, "I want to become a speech and drama teacher!" Good questions can be great at moving people forward.

I was slowly realising that I was a round peg in a square hole at work. There were more limited opportunities for women in South Africa in the 90s, less in the engineering company where I worked, and even less for women who weren't engineers, no opportunities that I knew of in South Africa. As a strong vocal Irish woman, the language I used didn't always go down well with senior leaders, although I know I was beloved by my boss, the engineers and the factory workers where I visited and spoke to people as part of my role. I had a wonderful manager in the beginning who taught me much about effective spoken communication in the corporate world, where email was growing fast as a form of internal and external communication. "Go and take a walk" was probably his best advice and I'm sure we accomplished so much more and saved time in walking to the other end of the company to speak with engineers than was accomplished via email, by others.

But within two years of his departure, I almost caused a bombastic consultant to have an apoplectic fit when I spoke truth to power in my first and last executive meeting. When they blamed the factory workers for a productivity problem that I believed was caused by ordering failures earlier in the cycle, I should not have begun with, 'There is a Greek expression which says, a fish rots from the head down'! A director who appreciated my insight agreed with me and turned things around, but it was so tiring battling to have a voice in a space where there was so little equality. That I was sitting in a Laura Ashley-type maternity dress didn't help my power look! I suppose a measurement of my 'misfit status' was in my last-ditch attempt to consider the company's potential to accommodate me at management level. Recognising the glass ceiling for women in an engineering company, I described myself as 'a flea in a jam jar' to the extreme consternation of the MD, in a one-to-one! Flowery analogies were right up there with flowery dresses in those times and that environment. I like to think I learnt as much about what *not* to do in the corporate world, as what *to* do in those days. On a high note, I did bring to light a massive embezzlement scheme in the company; I knew discretion when it was needed and was never associated with its uncovering.

And so, I became a drama student again for four years, taking Trinity College London teaching diploma exams. Much of what I learnt then formed the basis of my teaching and my voice and speech coaching under Joan Lee in Johannesburg, in preparation for the written and practical exams. Although Joan was Jewish, she confirmed that the Bible, as well as a dictionary and the *Complete Works of Shakespeare* were three compulsory books to have. I didn't question why, as I believe the first contains an extraordinary history of humans, poetry and stories, the second as we need to understand what we read and hear, and the third because Shakespeare covers every story type – history, tragedy, comedy and romance – so brilliantly. She was intimidating, excellent and got me through my first exams with flying colours, no mean feat with a 70% pass rate and a breastfeeding baby in tow. The next step involved becoming a member of the South African Guild of Speech and Drama Teachers (now the SA Academy) and I needed a minimum of English 1 in addition to my TCL qualifications. I studied remotely at UNISA, The University of South Africa, where the one week of lectures took place in Pretoria when my daughter was eight days old.

Two teachers later and a move to the UK and I submitted the thesis, gaining a Licentiate to teach Speech and Drama. Both teachers were outstanding and served me well for that stage in my studies. There is nothing quite like gut instinct and chemistry to help you decide who to work with. I use it in my work today, and still interview every client before agreeing to move forward. Relationships are precious and life is too short to make the wrong choices. Effective spoken communication doesn't happen if either the audience or the speaker is with the wrong person or people.

Becoming a speech and drama teacher

Within five years, I was fully qualified, having held down a full-time, then contract job with the engineering company. Before leaving for the UK and while still studying, I had my second, then third child while opening the doors of my first speech and drama studio, known as Blarney Studio, and ran workshops, groups and private lessons. It was hard work and full of challenges, but I was thriving and living my purpose. I never claimed to prepare anyone for fame and fortune: the focus of Blarney Studio, SA, was to teach children, teenagers and adults to fulfil their purpose through engaging with confidence. Because of my strong business background whilst growing up and working in the corporate world, I interviewed every candidate from aged seven upwards. I started my students at aged seven as I believe that pedagogically, children younger than this learn best through mostly self-directed play.

Marketing my studio was a joy and my motto, which has never changed, was born at this time,

Introduction

"Never underestimate your ability to enhance and influence the lives of others."

You now know a little bit about me running my studio and how I got there, but how did I switch from being a corporate worker to solopreneur and from student to teacher? Not easily, and most of the challenge was mindset-related and depended on being surrounded by the right and wrong people!

Through highly serendipitous circumstances, I resigned my full-time role in March 2000 and stayed on to deliver a 25-hour week contract for six more months. This was miraculous in South Africa, where women's rights were very much behind the times. I spent the rest of the year building up the business that was Blarney Studio. Being able to gradually transition was ideal and helped me to let go of one world while growing in confidence in the other.

But the biggest nudge to open my own studio came from a stranger called Kathy Robinson. As a drama teacher in her own right, she attended a concert at the Johannesburg branch of Trinity College London where certificates and diplomas were presented to that year's candidates and those who achieved top marks in each category were asked to perform their pieces. Because I had managed to get the top mark in the Licentiate Diploma category, I was asked to perform. Slightly embarrassed, I explained to the audience that I was hoping to become a teacher and was not a performer. I would therefore do my comedy piece. On the way to refreshments, Kathy grabbed my arm and whispered, "When are you going to open your studio?" I was again embarrassed.

"I don't know. I'm not ready yet."

"You must," she responded. "You'll be really good."

"Why"? I asked.

"Because you know it's not about you."

This was a valuable lesson that I've attempted to pass on to every student and client who comes through my doors. You will be good when it's not about you; it's about your audience. You'll read more about this concept later. But Kathy and I became friends and she mentored me over the coming months and encouraged me to go for it. I am grateful that she spoke up that day. I don't know when I would have had the courage to transition from being a free assistant for my drama teacher and she certainly wouldn't have had the incentive to encourage me to spread my wings.

And so, with a few workshops and poetry soirees under my belt in 2000, a full-time replacement was found at my corporate job, and I started interviewing for students for Blarney Studio. I can still remember my amazement as I closed the door behind the first nine-year old and his parents, that people believed in me and trusted me with their child. I was 32 and there was no way this would have happened had I come out of Trinity College, Dublin at 22 with a degree in Drama. As the four group lessons and private lessons started filling up, I grew in confidence and excitement for what was happening.

Lo and behold, I was a drama teacher, long before Amy Cuddy[4] coined the term 'Fake it 'til you become it!'

Becoming a voice and speech coach

Armed with many of the tools and techniques you'll find in the pages of this book, I set forth on my quest to help people across a broad range of demographics to fulfil their potential in communicating with confidence through speech and drama lessons.

Over the course of the next 14 years, I crafted lessons every week that were bespoke to the age and stage of the students and for the group or individual I was teaching. Some students came for both group and private lessons and we worked towards Trinity College London exams. My advertisements for the studio also attracted enquires from adults who wanted to grow in confidence or learn about effective spoken communication. Through the interview process, I realised I could help them too. In my third year, I was approached by a small private secondary school[5] to do drama a few hours a week and by a company in Gauteng to teach previously disadvantaged people to effectively communicate in person and on the telephone. The latter was due to a government scheme in South Africa which meant that 10% of company payroll went to the government, a bit like tax. To reclaim it, a company had to spend an equivalent amount upskilling previously disadvantaged people in post-Apartheid South Africa. Had we stayed in South Africa, this would have been a growing part of Blarney Studio work. I thoroughly enjoyed my term doing this, but we made a choice to move overseas, giving my husband an opportunity to do what I had done 13 years before and experience life in a new country.

Looking back, I realise that I was already doing coaching work at the Gauteng company and with private adult clients. However, when I rebranded as 'M A D Studio – Making A Difference' in Didcot, South Oxfordshire, I knew little about the British culture and had a lot to learn. Children and teenagers were an easy transition but after one term of adult classes I realised that a) adults in the UK have a lot less time for hobbies, and b) amateur dramatics is virtually free in the UK. Marketing was also far tougher and so I focused on young people and helped adults that approached me via word of mouth.

In 2008, alongside running my studio, I had an opportunity to work at a secondary school in a support capacity and it was there I received valuable training for Special Education Needs (SEN) including Dyslexia, Dyspraxia, ADD and ADHD as well as Conflict Management and Conflict Resolution. These courses have proved invaluable for considering clients and audiences with SEN and the latter two a foundation in delivering training on managing difficult relationships in the workplace. A two-year stint as Teacher of English, the first year full-time, reminded me of the many skills involved in creating good content which would help in creating and providing feedback on speeches for clients even today.

As a result of this English teaching post, I made the decision to not market my studio and let it quietly die. However, when word of mouth referrals came my way, I picked them up when a new Head of English was appointed at the school, and I was given an opportunity to step back. I was also approached by a local company to deliver training for them, and I had to admit that my real passion lay outside a curriculum-imposed classroom and my desire for working with adults had grown. But nothing had been wasted.

During this time, I had also worked for a charity and discovered that my communication skills and extraversion meant that I had built up a strong local network over the years and I was evidently good at networking. When I faced the reality that my real passion and purpose was to use my voice and speech coaching skills to help businesspeople, I knew I had to give it my full-time attention. It coincided fortuitously with my now older teenagers leaving school and attending university or college.

I loved the confidence and freedom that drama skills had given me as a teenager and how this could be transferred to everyone I taught. My work has always had equipping people for life as its primary focus. If you can speak and move with confidence, communicating your expertise will flow more freely into the world around you.

I also believe effective communication creates more equality in life. Too many of our institutions and governments are run by the privately educated privileged, who have been raised to speak and debate at an advanced level. It's time to level the playing field and in my sphere of influence, with the help of this book, I hope to do the same.

Effective communication is as much about listening as it is about speaking, perhaps even more so. The challenge I had was that 'teacher' and 'adult' don't go well together. 'Coach' was the most obvious fit, as watching and listening to clients before responding was key to selecting and delivering the best tools for their requirements. I was very fortunate to share my challenge with a respected leadership coach in one of my networks. She introduced me to and gifted me a copy of the book, *Time to Think* by Nancy Kline.[6] In Section Five, you'll read about this methodology and how it can help you too. I didn't realise when I started what a great gift this coaching style would be, but over the next four years I completed three courses and qualified as a Time to Think Certified Coach. I believe this has helped me to bring some wonderful tools and techniques together for Breathtaking Communication. Before that, you will have discovered all I believe you need to know: where to begin, how to be heard, how to keep people engaged and the external to that, add value.

I start with developing 'below the waterline' skills. These begin with breathing and relaxation and postural support. Breath connection, vocal resonance, breath control and projection are developed from here. These are foundational and covered in Section Two. Once the body and breath have the skills to support the voice, we can focus on making the most of our vocal skills in communication: modulation, articulation and accent. This is covered in Section Three.

As the opportunities now arise to speak with power, clarity and confidence, we also need to ensure that our content is well organised and also well delivered. Section Four ensures that your preparation is optimised through your processes of planning and practise and use of human and physical resources around you. This helps you consider what you need in both an in-person and online setting.

Is there more that you may need? Maybe. I've shared what I've learned about slides, props and notes, so that if you choose to use them, you will learn best practise, according to the latest thinking. Additionally, I've found it invaluable to have a philosophy around how I show up in my speaking, meeting engagements and work. I've shared mine with you in Section Five. You may want more, but at that point, it's over to you. I hope you will, by then, have the confidence to make the right decisions for your audience and your message.

This book is designed to be a toolbox you can dip into as you need. You don't have to read it from front to back, but it might be helpful to do at least the exercises in Section Two so that you have a firm foundation in place.

Now, as I say to all my speakers before their important engagements – enjoy!

Fiona Brennan-Scott, April 2022

Glossary of Terms

Articulation is the formation of clear and distinct sounds in speech.

Breath Control allows the delivery of a complete phrase, without interruption to take a breath, to make sense of a phrase or sentence. It is the very foundation of effective speaking, as it is the control of the outgoing breath that gives us voice.

Emphasis is the way of making a word or phrase stand out to bring out a certain meaning in a sentence. It can be achieved through an increase or change in one or a combination of the following; tone volume, inflection, pause, repetition and gesture.

Enunciation is the use of vowels and consonants such that your audience can understand you.

Inflection can be defined as the gentle rise and fall of the voice on syllables. We can inflect up (rising) and falling, compound rising and falling, and circumflex rising and falling.

Modulation is the means by which we change and vary the voice in order to engage our audience. Without modulation, the voice can be described as monotonous or boring. Modulation includes pitch, pace, pause and phrasing, inflection, emphasis and tone.

Pace is how quickly or slowly we speak, and it goes hand in hand with pitch.

A Pause is a short silence or a cessation in speaking. There are various types of pauses, a sense or grammatical pause is used to make sense of the sentence or the passage and is associated with phrasing.

A Phrase is a group of connected words, which may or may not contain a verb, but makes sense; a **phrase** is a group of words which form a grammatical unit.

Pitch is the height or depth of sound and is created by the vibration of air through our vocal cords. It is a product of length X mass. Changes in pitch are due to differing rates of vibration of the vocal cords. The human voice has a range of about two octaves. The vocal cords tighten when the pitch is raised, and vibrations increase and loosen when the pitch is lowered, and vibrations are fewer.

Pronunciation is how words are stressed using enunciation.

Public Speaking is engaging in spoken communication with three or more people where you are the primary speaker.

Resonance is the enlargement of the basic tone in the resonators (or hollow cavities) in the breath system - the front of the mouth and face, the throat and the chest.

Resonator Scale is formed of the words HOOT, HOOK, HOE, HAWK, HOCK, HARD, HUT, HIRT, HEARD, HAD, HEAD, HAY, HID, HEED. Mnemonic: Who would know aught of art must first learn and then take his ease.

Speech is the means by which a person expresses thoughts and feelings in words, which are produced by the formation of vowels and consonants.

Tone is the general quality of the voice and is produced in the resonators. It comprises *tone amount*, which is the volume of our speech and *tone colour*, which is the quality of speech.

Vocal variety is how the voice changes or modulates in speech for effective engagement.

Voice is the instrument of speech. It is produced by the vibration of air through the vocal cords.

Volume is the loudness made by the strength of the breath force.

Glossary of Terms[1]

SECTION ONE

Breath-taking Communication:
How does it work?

Chapter 1
Where Do You Begin?

Starting with purpose: the difference between talking and speaking

To quote Maria from *The Sound of Music*, "Let's start at the very beginning, it's a very good place to start."[1] For many of us, we began neurotypical life by expressing ourselves verbally. The traditional image of birth in films shows a doctor holding a baby upside down and slapping it on the bottom so it cries out. If it did, the doctor considered their job done. If the baby did not communicate in this way, a flurry of activity ensued as either the baby's life was in danger, or the baby was not healthy.

What is my point? We are considered to have arrived, not just when we are physically in the room, but when our voice has been heard. The doctor would know the breath-force of the baby was functioning adequately when it was able to power its voice. All that really changes from this point onwards is that we learn to use words to communicate, as at some point, calling out or screaming doesn't generally get us what we want. Therefore, our original purpose in using our voice is to demonstrate that we are healthy, and that we are here. If you are reading this, congratulations! You are a survivor. But are you thriving?

Given the right circumstances, we should thrive as communicators. Our purpose in communicating is to get what we need to survive and in the right environment, to thrive.

Ironically, things can start going wrong with our communication when we go to school. We are managed often by one person, in a large group. In most school settings, we are encouraged to spend a large portion of time listening and being quiet. Reading and writing are added to our skillset, and, for this, we are put sitting at a desk. Engaging in writing wasn't always comfortable, especially if we were left-handed and reading wasn't always a relaxing activity while we were learning.

Core Postural Physiotherapist, Mannie Babington Smith taught me that core posture should be at the heart of what we learned to do at school it isn't. As a result, we learned discomfort in communicating. Ideally, in a school environment, we should learn how to stand and sit in a way that maximise our body and breath for communication, adjusting the desk and chair, paper and books to work for our bodies, and not adjusting our bodies for them. The minor contortions that we often learnt by adjusting to our environments go some way to inhibit the remarkable body we have from thriving in spoken communication. The cave people drew on rocks, but for children in schools, paper is often put in front of them a certain way and we're taught to hold writing instruments a certain way. So many of us bent, twisted and turned to conform to what was expected of us and so our bodies suffered even as we sought to communicate.

That's the physical aspect. Added to this, is the behaviour that was expected, being told 'sit still', 'be quiet', 'you're very loud', 'speak up', 'he doesn't say much'. All of these add up; whatever we were told about how we showed up and used our voices by those in authority, affects us deeply. There's a physiological response. If it was all affirming or worked in our favour, we thrived and were encouraged and were then more likely to flourish in communication.

Our next challenge in communication arrives with puberty and the teenage years. Things happened in our body that we didn't always understand, and we certainly couldn't control. Bits grew. You grew.

Adults and peers passed remarks, or you just felt deeply uncomfortable in your skin. You slouched. You walked with your eyes down. Your voice broke, you muttered, or you didn't speak unless you had to. The purpose for some was to become invisible, to not be noticed. Your voice pulled back to settle in your throat and there it stayed, skulking in the shadows. The jaw tightened.

At this point, you can see that several circumstances have possibly worked against a person speaking out with power and confidence.

There can be other layers that block our ability to thrive in spoken communication. For me, it was my teeth. A well-meaning family friend suggested to my parents I would need braces. At 13, I was brought to a big city where an orthodontist with a gleaming smile and a few gold fillings took photos and exclaimed, "What a dreadful smile!" I already thought I was ugly compared to my friends and that at least I could be friendly and smile at people. Apparently not! I hope that breed of practitioner has all but died out. I hope you haven't had a comparable experience; unfortunately, many of us have.

And, like Sleeping Beauty surrounded by cobwebs and thorny trees, there goes our full potential, the full potential of our body and our voice to express our message loud and clear to the world. We may find our purpose academically, romantically, and spiritually, but unless we've been grown in very special soil, we will never really find our true voice and full purpose and potential until we reclaim the use of that beautiful pre-five body and voice.

My hope is to be your equivalent of a Fairy Godmother and release your body and voice from the tangles and snares that have held you back. Not using shears or bulldozers, but tools and techniques that will release you from whichever tower you're trapped inside. And in these pages, I will pass them to you one by one, so that you can release yourself and walk into a new place in your spoken communication.

You will hear me refer to voice throughout this book. I think of voice with a small 'v' as that which is formed in the throat and mouth. Then there's Voice with a capital 'V', your identity; it's your vocal fingerprint that expresses itself when you express your thoughts and feelings with your body and voice. For simplicity, I will write voice. Please consider both as you read.

You already have expertise

Before we proceed, may I suggest that you already have expertise? Like me as a child sitting in the theatre, you've already gathered many skills and techniques to help you on this journey. You're probably an expert audience member. You know what works and doesn't work. In your very core you respond positively or negatively to how people engage with you and others around you. In life as truly, if not more truly than on stage, our response to people is visceral.

If this does not resonate with you, it might be that you struggle with empathy or are autistic. It's helpful for audience engagement to develop awareness of people and their responses. This can be developed through time spent listening to and watching people, tuning in to what response, connection and engagement look and feel like. Without this understanding, we struggle to engage positively with people on a level that serves them and us. It appears to come naturally to some; it can be learned to varying degrees by others.

What do audiences deserve?

So, what do you deserve as you watch and listen to a speaker? At least the value of your ticket if you're at a paid event. And if you're not paying, it's still costing you your time and the opportunity to be elsewhere. I would suggest that audiences deserve to be respected by the speaker.

As speakers, we owe it to our audiences to not only be prepared and practise our material, but to deliver it in a way that is engaging. Otherwise, send an email, publish a paper or write a blog. There are a multitude of ways to reach audiences without expecting them to sit and listen. If you do show up to speak, make it worthwhile for everyone.

Later, in Section Five I go into more detail on the components of a Thinking Environment[©]; place, where and how we show up, need to say, 'You matter'.[2] If it matters enough for people to come and listen to us, and for us to show up to be heard, we need to show that speaking and listening matter.

Priority Order; speaker, message, audience?

The process of effective spoken communication begins by examining our priorities. This applies equally to meetings and any other public speaking opportunities.

For the purposes of public speaking, I believe an audience of at least three needs to be present. It's at that point the dynamic changes sufficiently for public speaking to kick in. A dialogue or conversation is a more suitable method of communication between two to three people

Fig 1

Looking at this diagram (Fig 1), the figure on the left is the speaker, the speech bubble is the message and the figures on the right are the audience.

Knowing that all three are important, essential even, for spoken communication to take place, consider or write next to each one which you believe to be *most* important in terms of first, second and third –

speaker, message or audience? What do *you* prioritise in how you approach such an opportunity?

Over the years, I have had shy or introverted people believe that it's most important for them to sort out their nerves and their fears as all eyes are on them. In their case, Speaker is number one. I've had others, particularly in STEM[3] who believe the subject matter is the top priority, therefore Message is number one. Those in more people-facing industries guess that it's Audience but would be the first to admit that their preparation for public speaking hasn't always reflected this as they put themselves or the product they are selling first.

I wonder what you thought. In truth, your highest priority must be the Audience, from the moment you are invited to speak, to when you've finished. I'm reminded of Covey's Habit Two of *7 Habits*[4] - 'Begin with the End in Mind'. When we speak to one person, how we speak is shaped by who they are. For example, speaking to someone in finance about a new product will have a different emphasis to speaking to someone in marketing. Speaking to an experienced colleague will assume more than speaking to a recent recruit. It's the same with a group: what do you know about the audience that will help you shape the best message? If you can't possibly know, what can you assume? At the very least, you should be able to assume they're interested in your message or being there, but even that might be a stretch at times.

What can you do then to ensure that they are drawn in?

I can guarantee that if you keep your audience front and centre from the time you sit down to plan your content, you will have a greater chance of success and engagement. An audience can tell when you're thinking of them, in the same way a child can tell if a parent is really paying attention. If you can't think of everyone, and this will often be the case, think of the group that will benefit most from hearing your message. If it helps, write down a few notes about them, even draw a figure, I favour a gingerbread person. Write what you can about them on their torso and stick it somewhere prominent during your preparation so you can look at them when searching for the right words, phrase or analogy.

It follows on logically then, that the next most important element is Message. When you know who your audience is, it will be far easier to shape your message for them. No longer is it about you or what you know, you now start to ask questions, such as:

- What do they need to know?
- What response do I want to elicit? What do I want them to think, do and/or feel as a result of this message?
- What, therefore, do I need to say and what do I need to leave out?
- How best can I communicate this?

It may even be at this point you realise that speaking in a meeting or a presentation is not actually the best means of communication, and that's fine. Rather find out now than sit down at the end of a talk, realising you made a mistake.

To the huge relief of the introverts and shy people, Speaker comes last. You are the humble messenger and at the same time, the vital communicator of it. With the right skills and techniques, you embody the message. How can you use your voice, your speech and your body to communicate this message to an audience in a way that engages them?

I've carried a picture of this which always comes to mind. I imagine a kingdom in the Middle Ages. The ruling monarch has a message they need to get to the villagers. It could be a celebration or news of an attack. Either way, it's vital that the message is clear, and the villagers know how to respond. The content of that message needs to be clear and concise. There needs to be no ambiguity as to whether the people need to clean up and dress up or reach for their pitchforks. The monarch writes on a scroll and hands it to you. You are the horseback envoy. The villagers cannot read. They are entirely dependent on you to understand the message. At what pace will you ride and how will you communicate that message? What will your facial expression communicate and how will your voice support that message?

You had better make darned sure they don't come to the party with pitchforks or get attacked with only their party clothes and good looks to defend them!

Let's see what we can do to get it right, shall we?

What do you need as the speaker?

If you have an audience and you have a message, what do you, as the Speaker need to make engagement happen?

Most of us aren't taught the skills in our educational system that will give us the confidence to do a great job of effectively engaging an audience. Some countries are better than others. It's easy to focus on external elements to help us or distract our audience, such as slides, props, appearance or information overload. But if we define skill as the ability to do something well, we need the tools and techniques to equip us. As we become skilled, we grow in confidence from the inside out and can draw on additional external aids that will enhance the message. When this confidence is present, we discover that we need very little else.

Chapter 2

How Can I Take Responsibility For My Part?

How to approach a public speaking opportunity

The position of a speaker is much like that of a leader; it involves taking responsibility for your part. To this end, you must ensure that your speech is fit for purpose, in both delivery and content. Consider to whom you are speaking, where and why. Is it a formal or informal occasion? This will influence your language, your content, your voice and your appearance. These are discussed in more detail later in the book. But before we get there, I believe it's worth thinking about expectations and assumptions.

Managing expectations

Your goal in managing expectations is to eliminate as many assumptions and unknowns as possible, knowing that there is always at least one curveball on the day. Believe me, there always is.

Public speaking opportunities can take many forms and since COVID-19, can be expected to take place online as much as in person. Here are some common opportunities my clients have come across over the years:

- Speaking in public spaces where three or more people gather including meetings, training, classes or lectures.
- Delivering speeches as part of an organisation such as Toastmasters International (TMI), the Professional Speaking Association (PSA) or for work.
- Sharing a one to two minute 'Elevator Pitch.'[1]
- Delivering a five to twenty-minute business talk at a Networking Event.
- Wedding or other religious gatherings.
- Interviews.
- Speaking on video for websites or social media.
- Sports coaching.
- Performance (e.g., magician, Master of Ceremonies/compere).
- Television appearances.

Our needs and expectations for each of these can differ vastly. As I considered expectations, I realise that many may be based on assumptions of which we're not even conscious. Here are two you may have, with suggestions on how to manage them to increase your likelihood of success.

A baseline expectation: To be listened to without interruption

One expectation for all of them may be that we will be listened to without interruption, that we will be given a hearing. Even this can be an assumption, especially if we're not given equality in society because of one or more characteristic, e.g., age, gender, race, accent. But we can create an expectation that we will be listened to in how we show up and that is something you can control. As speakers, we cannot control others, but we can influence them.

To meet this expectation: stand, smile, make eye contact with your audience and wait at least two seconds before you begin.

Unless you are sure you can be seen by everyone in the room, and unless no one ever stands to speak in this context, standing will ensure you are seen. This is considerate. Smiling says you are pleased to be addressing the audience and puts people at ease. Making eye contact ensures that you are engaging with your audience and increases the likelihood that they will engage with you. Pausing allows them time to give you their attention before you speak.

If I am asked to speak at an event, I have a process I follow and recommend this to you. Some of these may not be relevant but if you create a checklist, it's easy to eliminate what is not applicable for your particular situation. It can be more frustrating to forget something you should have considered.

An unhelpful baseline assumption: the speaker at an event has high status

There is a baseline assumption I would like to deal with: you may consciously or unconsciously believe that the speaker at an event has high status. Several factors may contribute to this:

- You have given speakers high status as they stand on a stage or are in the proverbial spotlight on or offline and you sit amongst the minions in the audience.
- They seem important because of their confidence and knowledge.
- Their name is written in a programme and/or in the advertising.
- They are applauded after their talk and given a lot of attention.
- At a live event, they may be seated at a more prestigious table.

The problem with this assumption, whether true or untrue, is that it can lead us to believe that we will be looked after, or our needs will be met in a way which will disappoint at best. At worst, it will result in us not being able to deliver well because we don't have what we need to deliver our best work. In my experience, unless the speaker is rich, famous or both, most speakers must organise quite a lot, even if that is done by their staff. On the day or night of the event, most organisers are focused on the attendees and the last thing they need is a speaker placing expectations or demands on them.

To meet this expectation: good advance planning is vital – before the attendees arrive. This will also raise your status at the event and garner respect from those around you.

Apart from this, it's important to have a process that will eliminate assumptions so that you can have realistic expectations. You will then be better prepared to consider what might be done if that expectation is not met on the day. This is research and planning on a macro scale. Planning and researching the speech itself will be dealt with in Chapter 17; some of it will be informed by the macro research below.

Know the task

Stephen Covey in, *7 Habits of Highly Effective People* includes 'Begin with the end in mind'. Ensure you understand the speaking task from the person inviting you to speak. This includes the audience profile and the overall theme of the event. What are they hoping to accomplish by having you speak? What do the organisers hope the audience will think, feel or do as a result of your talk or speech? This may be quite fluid, depending on whether it's an internal or external presentation, and your position as an expert in your field. Sometimes you may be answering these questions for yourself, but it's always beneficial to consult the person who's paying your fee or seeks to benefit from having you there.

On the other hand, you may be requested to speak to a topic, and this requires clarity from the organisers. Find out if you will be introduced or need to do that yourself. It's often requested but if not, offer to provide an introduction for the host. This will ensure it's what you'd like to hear, and they often appreciate the consideration as they then don't have to create one from scratch. I've mostly been fortunate but have had the extremes of a terrible and inaccurate introduction as well as one so glowing that I didn't know how I could live up to it!

A cautionary tale: Recently, I was at a conference when delegates complained that one speaker in a breakout session used the entire session as an opportunity for a sales pitch. It's easy to think that if you're not being paid, it's fair to take the opportunity to promote what you do. But if you share your expertise and offer your details, potential clients will be naturally attracted to you and want more. Wisdom in this area is paramount as I'm certain that this speaker failed in three ways:

- He did not engage his audience positively
- He did not succeed in his selling goal
- He will not be asked back or recommended to or by others.

Have an onsite liaison person

Have a go-to liaison person you can coordinate with at the venue who will answer your questions in the lead up to the event. This may be the person who is hiring or inviting you, but it may be a person they have delegated or an identified Events Coordinator. This person will be your greatest ally so be kind to them! Introduce yourself and get their card or name and number. Establish with them in advance that they are happy to coordinate with you about anything to do with the event so that you can ensure the audience have the best possible experience. This is not about you being a Primo Don or Prima Donna and once you have the attitude of serving your audience, you can communicate easily.

Plan to send this person a 'thank you' card after the event. Think about what you'd like to thank them for as that's what you need to ask for and expect!

Know the place

Find out what you can about the venue, as they say in movies, 'case the joint'. This includes considerations such as travel distance, traffic at the time of day you'll be travelling, parking if relevant and access.

If you know how much time this will all take, you can ensure you're there 15 to 30 minutes in advance.

Access includes such factors as whether you need to be collected from reception or if you need an access card, as well as any special considerations for your physical needs such as wheelchair access and appropriate toilet facilities. If practical, do a dry run to the venue and look out for any news in social media of events, road closures and weather conditions on the day which may cause delays. Check with your liaison person and communicate anything you've discovered which may help them or may impact attendance or start time. If a dry run is impractical for various reasons, you will be dependent on your liaison to provide you with this information and it's worth allowing more time in this case, including possibly the location of a nearby café if arriving too early would be inappropriate or a nuisance.

Know the space

Find out what you can about the space in which you'll present. If it's a physical meeting, where is it in the building? What are the noise levels and other distractions you may be competing with? How big is the space for the comfort of those attending and your delivery? If it's not covered by someone else, you will need to know the location of toilets and fire exits so that you can communicate this to the audience. Ideally, have someone else do this as it doesn't create an impactful start to your talk, but is considered standard for training after an engaging introduction.

For both virtual and physical events, how many people will be in the room and is this likely to vary? If you're speaking at a breakout session this may mean moving rooms and therefore you will need to be prepared for a large or small audience, depending on the other speakers and topics.

If you are intending to use slides for a presentation, what technology will you use and what will be provided to support this? Don't take anything for granted.

Even more so if you're going to another country. Check for technical compatibility: make sure you have connectors or adaptors to support the electric socket configuration used in your destination country. An extension lead is a standard part of my kit; this will ensure that all the plugs don't have to change.

For both virtual and physical meetings, sharing slides will require co-ordinating with the host, finding out if there's a producer and ensuring you have sharing rights. I would always send through any slides and a recording of the presentation in case of unexpected interruptions in Wi-Fi, but of course emphasise in advance the importance of you being there in person to answer questions. I tend to send them when everything has been confirmed and paid for, a maximum of 24 hours before the event. For paid speaking work, you should have a contract protecting your Intellectual Property (IP).

Regarding your delivery, there are more questions to answer. Will you be sitting or standing? The layout of the room may help inform this for in-person presentations. What will make your audience engage more effectively and can you be dynamic sitting down on a virtual call? Would a mixture work? From training experience, I have found that when I sit, having stood or moved around, the energy in the room drops. This is fine at certain stages of delivery, such as group discussion or reflection, as long as I can be seen by my audience. It is more challenging in the afternoon following lunch. You will hear this again, but your baseline responsibility as a speaker is to keep your audience awake! In 2020, I came to favour the energy of standing for online presentations, both for my own sake and the energy of the audience. But I do have a chair nearby for when I'm not presenting. Professional speakers who are wheelchair users and experienced speakers learn and know how to manage the energy levels in the room or virtual space effectively.

If you are standing to deliver your talk, you may need a podium. If this is not provided, think about how to manage your notes. At this point you just need to establish where or what you will be speaking from and if it's easily height adjustable. A decent quality music stand works well and doesn't act as barrier between you and the audience if positioned strategically.

The size of the space will also dictate the requirement for a microphone. If one is required, establish if it is provided by the venue and ensure that you can have a technical practise before you speak so that you are familiar with its workings. If you must provide your own, you will usually have to supply all the sound too. A space that does not provide a microphone usually does not need one and you will have gained the skills to project your voice into such a space in Section Two of this book. You are best advised to have a technical rehearsal if possible so that you can experience your voice in the space. If this is not possible, you will also learn the skills here to 'breathe the space' before you speak, and this may be the best you can hope for. There will be many occasions where being in the space in advance is not an option, interviews being an obvious example, but it is always good to ask where appropriate. Your liaison person can at worst say 'no'.

Do what you can to ensure seamless set up for a great first impression. It's true: you only get one chance to make a first impression.

Case study: Nancy Kline

Dynamic isn't always the highest calling for a speaker. Sometimes the goal is engagement alone. Nancy Kline is one of the most engaging speakers and trainers I've ever heard and received training from, both in person and online. I've never seen her stand to deliver, yet her engagement is virtually hypnotic because of the attention she gives. I believe this has a lot to do with the philosophy of a Thinking Environment© and therefore is congruent with her message.

What will serve your audience and message best? Experiment with both.

A word about managing time

This important consideration is dealt with in more detail later. However, lest you are picking this book up a week or two before you've been asked to speak, I'd like to briefly mention it here. Firstly, you will always need to spend more time than you imagine your favourite speaker does. Secondly, a speech or presentation consumes thinking time as well as dedicated time you've set aside for preparation. If your subconscious doesn't think you're adequately prepared, your body and mind will kick in to 'save you'. Our survival instinct doesn't want us to expose ourselves or put ourselves in a vulnerable place where we may get hurt. It's an instinct as old as humanity. This may lead to sleepless nights. I don't believe public speaking should be a life-shortening exercise and stress and sleeplessness can do this.

> *"If I am to speak ten minutes, I need a week for preparation; if fifteen minutes, three days; if half an hour, two days; if an hour, I am ready now."*
> Anonymous[2]

Asking how much time you need to prepare a 20-minute speech is very much a 'how long is a piece of string' question. Based on personal and client experience, if you are unfamiliar with public speaking, unfamiliar with the topic, unfamiliar with the venue and unfamiliar with the audience, I would encourage you to allow a minimum of 100 dedicated hours to prepare. If any one of the elements are familiar to you, you can take off some hours for each.

Don't assume a five-minute talk is any easier, as selecting what should be included and timing it to fit, can take a lot of time. There are instances when one can't dedicate a lot of time, such as a eulogy or an interview at short notice, but both parties know the circumstances and allowances are made. It's a pity to let yourself do less than your best otherwise, as a bad experience will diminish confidence and make it so much harder the next time.

Ideally, I like to work with clients for a minimum of twelve weeks before their speaking opportunity so that is probably a good rule of thumb if you have the luxury of allowing that much time.

Measuring for success

This is a good time to ask yourself 'How will I know if I've been successful?' Starting with the hoped-for outcome in mind ensures that you will know if and when you accomplish it or them.

Success criteria and desired outcomes may be fairly obvious with a job interview, but what about other public speaking opportunities? Our opinion, while important and valid, can be unreliable unless there is very obvious feedback, such as a standing ovation or people getting up and walking out! Spontaneous feedback from others can be equally unreliable as people are generally kind or will avoid saying anything at all. The feedback that really speaks louder than words, is a request to speak again, but those requests can take time to happen. It is therefore helpful to identify some criteria for success in advance of the talk, so that you can measure it afterwards.

In my initial discovery meeting with a client, I will ask them to identify what success will look like and make note of their response. When they stop, I will ask, 'And what else?' until they have finished. I suggest you do something similar as you approach your public speaking task. It is what you will return to when you reflect afterwards.

You could share some of your success criteria in advance with anyone giving you feedback, so that they understand what matters to you. Although some of your outcomes may be private, monetary and long-term, so it's possibly best to retain that for your own reflection. But do have those measurement criteria in mind as you go into any speaking engagement.

SECTION TWO

How do I do it?

Chapter 3
Assumptions and Learning about Learning

We all operate from a place of assumption. For the purpose of this chapter, I'm going to assume that you have purchased this book because you want to have tools and techniques to communicate, like the leader or subject matter expert you want to be. That's a fair assumption, considering the book title. I'm also going to assume that your goal is to engage with power and confidence. That engagement could be with a live audience or to a camera, and in the case of the latter, it could be live or for broadcasting later. The exercises in this section will help you to accomplish this. While it's focused on your spoken communication, don't be surprised if you raise your game in all areas of communication because of the transferable tools and techniques you acquire.

I cannot know how experienced you are at public speaking as you read this book, but I can assume that your experience has left you feeling less than competent for the task. Even confident speakers can freeze or burn when speaking in person or to a camera. Talking to a piece of equipment is not natural; I am writing this book to help you make it look like it is. That's what professional means to me for many things – effortless accomplishment.

Chapter 3

As a child, I watched professional snooker players make the game look simple and easy. When I was old enough to reach the table and play for myself, I realised how hard it was. It takes discipline and hours of hard work to make most 'games' in life look like effortless accomplishment. It is the same for public speaking, although, we've all been able to speak since we were small.

Using snooker as an illustration is not a bad idea, not just because it's virtually the only sport I grew up watching on TV, but because the focus and pace of the game is comparable to the delivery of a good talk – practised, planned, considered and measured in a situation where you are working alone at the point of delivery and all eyes are on you as you 'give it your best shot'. As an aside, snooker is a popular spectator sport to watch on TV, possibly because all the action takes place on a table that fills a camera lens quite comfortably. There might be a lesson to learn here about being easy to watch for our audience.

My plan in this section is to not only take you through a series of foundational exercises that I believe are fundamental to public speaking but also create a body and voice that are ready to engage with an audience.

My hope is that you will try all the exercises and I guarantee that if you engage with them fully, you will experience the benefits and succeed in gaining confidence in public speaking. This might be a good time to formulate your own effective communication goal, if you've not done so already. Make it big and bold. You might want to use my favourite example of a goal in this John F. Kennedy quote:

> *"I believe that this Nation should commit itself to achieving the goal, before this decade is out, of landing a man on the moon and returning him safely to earth."* [1]

Decide: who is going to do the public speaking, in what role or capacity, and with what support? What are you going to do specifically? When are you going to do it by?

Now it's your turn.

My goal for public speaking as a result of engaging with this book:

- What? To…
- When? By…

Section One focuses on what I refer to as 'below the waterline' techniques. No one needs to see you doing them, but they will experience the benefits when you present.

Do you know how you learn best? An introduction to VARK

As a starting point, it is helpful to consider how you best engage with learning. When you've been most successful at learning, what was happening? How was the information being delivered? It's important to be mindful of your own learning style because it will dictate your preferences. It's also important for you to understand that everyone is a different combination of these preferences because that will motivate you to cater to your audiences' needs.

Does hearing something a few times help? Do you need to see information? Do you need to repeat or copy what you're learning? Does making notes, in words or pictures, help? Or do you like to read or watch related videos around the subject? The truth is that we all have an optimal way of learning.

I would like to introduce you to VARK. Neil D. Fleming and Coleen E. Mills identified in a 1992 study that students have four different ways of learning: visual (seeing), auditory (hearing), reading and writing, and kinaesthetic (doing/experiencing). Basically, we all have learning preferences that are a combination of the four and within that, some are stronger than others. If you learn in a combination of these learning styles and your audience does too, it makes sense to cater for that in your talk.

There are free VARK questionnaires available online if you are keen to find out your learning preferences, but here is a summary of what you might find under each area:[2]

Visual

A highly visual learner likes to see information pictorially displayed - maps, diagrams such as mind maps or spider diagrams, graphs, charts, flow charts, etc. You get the picture? Visual learners might say, more accurately, do you get the graphics?!

Auditory

Auditory learners prefer information that is heard or spoken.

Auditory is about hearing, so learners with this as their primary preference generally learn best from podcasts, radio, audiobooks, lectures, group discussion, email, mobile phone exchange, speaking, webchat and talking things through. A person with aural preference will enjoy talking out loud as well as to themselves. They are possibly external processors too – thinking aloud, rather than sorting out their ideas before speaking. They often learn by repeating what they hear or by asking questions.

Reading/Writing

Fleming added the 'R' to what was previously VAK. I tend to believe that much of what this includes is covered in VAK already because I find the process of note-making and taking quite a kinaesthetic activity, but see what you think for yourself.

Reading/Writing learners prefer information displayed as words. Literacy is highly valued by employers of graduates and emphasises text-based input and output in all its forms. Because it's important to create and operate in a sustainable environment, it's important to make these options available to everyone, so that people who don't have 'R' as a preference can have access to them, while High 'R's can print them out and write in or on them: manuals, reports, and handouts. Essays and assignments fall into this category too and are the bread and butter of learning for teachers and students. Diaries or journals, dictionaries, the Internet, PowerPoint, lists, quotations, and thesauri really matter to this learning preference group.

Kinaesthetic

Kinaesthetic means "relating to a person's awareness of the position and movement of the parts of the body by means of sensory organs (proprioceptors) in the muscles and joints".[3] The briefest and best definition I know is 'learning by doing'. This will include watching people do demonstrations, filmed activity, simulations, videos, as well as case studies, practise, and applications of what people have done or are doing. Note, the films and videos need to be of real things, situations, and people; the illustration must be concrete and often multi-sensory. Writing or speaking kinaesthetically can work if it's strongly based in reality. Strong kinesthetics would refer to themselves as practical and be recognised for this.

Why might these learning preferences be important to a speaker? To illustrate by example, I'm a strong visual and kinaesthetic learner. If I don't consider that my audience has a combination of people with different learning styles, I'm highly likely to focus on visual and kinaesthetic. For me, this means I will either use props or have slides with images to support what I'm saying. I will also ask my audience to engage in an exercise, as kinaesthetic learners learn by doing. People in my audience who learn better by reading and audio may struggle to tune in. Catering for all learning preferences means I'm going to take responsibility for ensuring that I'm either providing written handouts or putting key words and points on slides to reinforce what I'm saying to my audience. I will also use vocal variety and pause to appeal to the auditory learners. Pace will also ensure that notes can be made, and handouts will provide space for this. For this reason, I would make the handouts optional as it's wasteful for someone who's not going to find it useful and, in some cases, I may choose to communicate that they're provided afterwards.

Sensitivity to VARK will influence the choices I give people. Non-kinaesthetic learners may cringe at the thought of engaging in an exercise, so if appropriate I will make the exercise voluntary or discreet. But as non-participants in a room can create self-consciousness for others, I would rather motivate everyone to get involved. Conversely, if you score strongly on the 'R' in VARK, it may help to take notes after you've engaged with the exercises in each section. What's important to you will stand out. If it's easier, record what you remember or, tell a friend or family member. Work with your VARK style to guide you.

You will find VARK weaves its way organically into the section on presentation skills, under tools and props, and the benefits of understanding and considering VARK will become clearer.

Why learning gets worse before it gets better

Before you read the next chapter, where we will explore exercises to prepare you for public speaking, I'd like to introduce you to the Four Stages of Learning. It is a model of change and growth which explains the process you'll go through as you learn. This is to encourage you because some of what you learn to do isn't going to seem natural or organic, which contradicts my commitment to help you become a more authentic version of yourself.

The four stages of competency or the Four Stages of Learning is a key tool in the process of learning and improving skills. It was developed at Gordon Training International by Noel Burch in 1970, expanding on Martin M. Broadwell's theory of the previous year. I like this model because it's simple, it's applicable to the way we learn and it's highly applicable to the process that I'm taking you through.

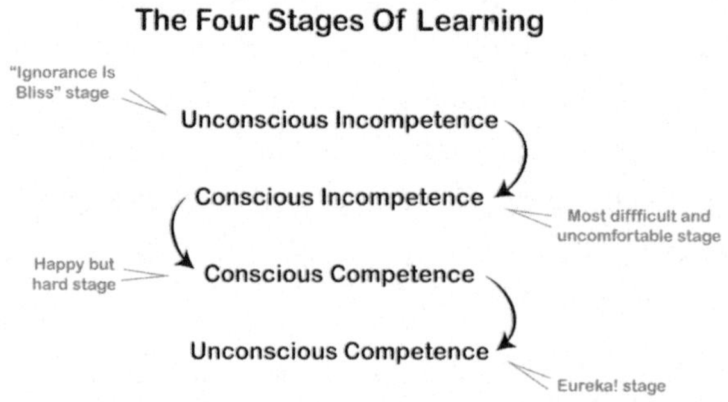

The Four Stages Of Learning

"Ignorance Is Bliss" stage

Unconscious Incompetence

Conscious Incompetence — Most diffficult and uncomfortable stage

Happy but hard stage — Conscious Competence

Unconscious Competence — Eureka! stage

Fig 2

26

When it comes to learning, we start off with **Unconscious Incompetence** (Fig 2). We don't know what we don't know. For example, if you're sitting in the passenger seat watching an adult drive, you might think, 'well, that looks easy'. It's possibly the same when you come to this book, having seen many competent speakers communicate effortlessly. You need help, you want help but wouldn't know where to start. But it looks easy, so it must be easy, right? At this stage, ignorance is bliss!

The next stage is **Conscious Incompetence**. Through learning you become aware of what you've been doing incorrectly and find out what to do correctly. You now know what you don't know. It's akin to sitting behind the wheel of a vehicle for the first time and realising there are pedals, indicators and mirrors and you really don't know where to start. This is an uncomfortable stage and in a way it's worse than ignorance. At this point in learning, people can give up, thinking 'I'm far better off without this'. Does that sound familiar? It's important to keep going through this phase and commit to learning because what's at the end is worth it - you as a competent, confident speaker!

The next stage is **Conscious Competence**. This is when you know what you have learnt but it's not embedded – you must consciously do everything according to what you've learned, you're trying it out for size. This would be equivalent to the first weeks and months of learning to drive where you must think about checking the mirrors, turning the key in the ignition, going into first gear, conscious of every step along the way. But you're driving – you're actually driving! It's still slightly uncomfortable in terms of stages but it's better and it's more empowered.

The fourth stage is what I call the Eureka Stage where we move into **Unconscious Competence**. This is when you know the techniques, you've practised them consciously and, bit by bit, you start doing them without even having to think about it - they have become you. For instance, I've been standing and walking in the Bespoken Technique of Posture so long now that I don't even have to think about it, but it took a while to get here. Sometimes when I'm in a situation where I don't need to be noticed, I get noticed and realise it's because I'm projecting power and confidence through my posture! Using the driving analogy, this stage is when you get in your car thinking, 'I'm going to the city/the meeting/work' and you don't give the process a second thought because you *are* a driver.

Please keep these in mind as you begin to apply the learning in this book. Fasten your seatbelt – you *will* be a Speaker by the end of this journey!

How to approach the exercises

You will find that the full benefits from the exercises in this section will be realised when they're done regularly. I recommend practise on alternate days, integrating them into an existing routine if possible. Studies have shown the importance of learning by doing[4] and this applies more so for kinaesthetic learners. Practicing the techniques will embed them; they will 'become' you.

This book is designed to be a toolbox you can dip into as you need. Through explaining what each idea or exercise will accomplish, I trust you will find the ones that you need most, and they will enhance your speaking performance.

Finally, please dress comfortably when you do the exercises as there will be some stretching, and movement involved.

Chapter 4
Where Do We Begin?

Freeing your body from tension

The most common question I'm asked as a voice coach is, 'How can I project my voice?' This question always calls to mind a story from Ireland about a tourist who pulls in beside a local walking along the road.

Winding down the window, the tourist asks, 'How do I get to Dublin?'

'Well,' says the local scratching his head, 'I wouldn't start from here.'

You see, when it comes to speaking, projection is the last thing that happens to the voice in the process of being heard well.

A Water Tip

The first tip I want to give you when speaking, is to have a glass of water handy. I always provide this for a face-to-face session. There are a few reasons for this:

1. It's the best lubricant for your vocal cords.[1]
2. If you're offered something to drink in an interview, it's easy for them to provide and better for your voice than anything else.
3. If you're stuck for something to say in a presentation or interview, pause and have a sip while you're thinking and regaining your composure.

lubricant for your vocal cords [1]

What do *you* think is the primary barrier for public speaking? If you thought tension or nerves, you guessed correctly. And what happens in the body when we experience tension caused by nervousness?

- The amygdala (the part of the brain where we process communication) is affected, which can cause 'a blank'.
- Our body tenses up and our breathing can become shallower.
- Our voice can become thin or shrill and lose power.
- As a result of this, we most definitely lose connection with our audience, who are the sole purpose of us speaking in the first place!

Therefore, the starting point has got to be relaxation. Even if you think your body is not affected by tension, it's still a good idea to check that you're not carrying any unconscious tension in your body so that you can maximise your physical and vocal potential to engage with your audience.

Consider the following: The *voice* is made in the voice box. The *breath* powers the voice. *Breath* is made in the lungs. The spine, the ribcage, in fact your whole *posture*, supports the lungs. Tension affecting any of these areas in the body will therefore affect the voice. It will also impact our body language, especially gesture and facial expression. Consequently, having a body which is free from tension and ready to communicate is vital for good public speaking.

Here are some exercises to help you complete a body check to ensure you're relaxed and free from unnecessary tension (we need some tension to stay upright!). Feel free to replace or substitute these with other exercises you may have in place that tick the boxes for you. Over the years, I've had martial arts clients, a dancer, a personal trainer and a movement coach who have complementary exercises in their practice. I just know the following are comprehensive for completing a body check; they're tried and trusted by myself and my clients over the years.

Exercise 1: Spine Stretch

Firstly, we're going to stretch the spine by reaching up, stretching your fingertips to aim for the sky, then:

- Breathe in through the nose on a count of three – stretch, reach, and relax as we breathe out through the mouth on one, two, three.
- Repeat twice more as we breathe in deeply and exhale slowly.

Why do we breathe in through the nose and out through the mouth? That's for several reasons – you'll get to realise that I like to have ulterior motives for everything I do!

- We warm the breath if we inhale through our nose.
- We don't dry out our mouth (important, because one of the things that happens if we're anxious about speaking is our mouth tends to dry up.)
- We catch any dust particles instead of breathing them in and potentially coughing.

Exercise 2: Neck Roll

A lot of tension we carry is carried in our upper body, the neck and shoulder region so it's vital to check and release that next.

- Drop your chin to your chest and roll your head to the left, across and up to your shoulder, and then down and right to the other shoulder. This is a boat-shaped roll. As you do this, you should feel the muscles stretching at the back of your neck and across your shoulders.
- Repeat twice. Ensure it's a roll and not a move – it takes tension to *move* but a roll will ensure a stretch while relaxing all the required muscles.

Make sure you do a semi-circle and not a circle. There's no need to stretch the muscles at the front of your neck. In fact, you could cause strain if you do.

I choose three repeats because doing or saying something three times reinforces it. Any less doesn't seem to stick and any more can seem unnecessary.

Exercise 3: Shoulder Roll

Next, we're going to release tension from the shoulders. We're going to work on one shoulder at a time but as you get into this exercise, and it becomes embedded you can just do both together.

- Imagine that there's a pencil sticking out from your shoulder and you're drawing a big circle on the wall, first forwards, completing a big circle.
- Rotate backwards. While you're doing this, relax your arm completely, try not to actively move your hand or your elbow, just letting them follow where the shoulder leads. This then becomes an isolation exercise which helps you realise the control you have of your body by raising awareness. It will help when you're practising delivery as you may become

aware of some unhelpful habits that were previously unconscious.[2]

- Rotate three times one way and three times the other.
- Repeat with the other shoulder. Again, three times one way and then three times the other. At this point, it doesn't matter which shoulder you start with and doesn't matter which direction you go in first.
- Now do them both together. Firstly, rotate forwards three times and then back three times.

I personally love this exercise; it feels like self-massage, and you should feel the tension being released from your shoulders. The reason I like to end on a backward roll is because when we finish, our posture is better than if we end with rolling forwards as it opens the chest more.

Exercise 4: The Lunge

The next exercise reminds me of fencing and I don't mean the kind that makes good neighbours (See Fig 3)! For this exercise, keep in mind that too much weight on the front leg can put a lot of pressure on the knee, and there's a risk that, by shifting your weight forward, you could flex the front knee too much and strain it.

Fig 3

- Come forward on the left leg in a comfortable lunge. Weight down in the pelvis, i.e., equally distributed between front leg and back leg. A balance tip from a dance teacher: imagine you have a third leg that goes down straight from the centre of your pelvis, between your two other legs, that's the one supporting your weight. That way, you're always straight on top of your centre of gravity.

- Front leg: knee is bent no more than 90^0 and never overshooting your toes.
- Back leg: knee bent, heel lifted, weight on the toes.
- Resting your left hand on your left leg for stability, rotate your right arm, firstly one way, about three times and then the other way, again three times. Feel the tension flowing out through your fingertips as you do this.
- Swap over and repeat on the other side.

The more enthusiasm with which you do this exercise, the more tension will be released from your body. However, all these exercises must be done to a point of release and not to a point of pain. Stop if you experience pain and check in with your doctor.

These exercises are quite simple and should be achievable by those in moderate to good health. Use a piece of furniture to support you if this gives you more confidence. I have adapted these exercises for wheelchair users in Chapter 9.

You should now be experiencing a body free from tension. Tune in and check.

The final step is about perfect posture for public speaking – standing or sitting correctly so that you look confident and are maximising your posture for breath support. Think of an athlete on the starting blocks for a race. The correct 'pose' gives them an advantage and the best chance of making a good start. And believe me, public speaking is a feat of athletic proportions!

Ideally, we should stand when presenting, if we are so able. This ensures our audience has the best possibility of seeing us – and you should now understand that it's about what works for the audience and not for us! But it does work best for us too, as we can engage the entire body in giving our voice strength and power.

At the time of writing this book, the business and even private world have spent many hours connecting and engaging with their audiences via a computer screen due to COVID-19 and the resulting lockdowns. However, even before the pandemic, many video presentations, small meetings, and interviews were conducted sitting down. If there are three to four people around a table and you can be seen and heard by everyone, this works well. I will therefore cover both seated and standing posture below so that you can maximise your spoken communication, depending on what the situation demands.

The positions below are what I call 'home' positions, from which you can move or gesture. I'm not suggesting people maintain them throughout a presentation – that would look and feel unnatural, but if it becomes your default position, it *will* maximise your appearance and breath for speaking. A certain amount of stillness gives a speaker presence.

Exercise 5a: Standing Posture

The Bespoken Technique of Posture maintains a standing posture that projects power and confidence to really engage your audience. I'm going to take it from the ground up.

- Stand with your feet about hip-width apart – two fists' worth of space.
- Knees not locked. If you lock them, you'll know what that feels like and just unlock them from there. Locking our knees leads to a tightening of the larynx, amongst other tightening.[3]
- Hips in line with the ankles – not sticking your tummy out, not sticking your bum out but nicely lined up.
- Shoulders in line with the hips – not a slump and not an army pose - just nicely stacked above the hips.
- Chin in line with your sternum. If you've never felt it before, find your sternum: it's the bone in the centre of the chest. When

the chin is in line with the sternum your chin is not sticking out and it's not pulled into a double chin.

- Next, lift your sternum slightly. This produces a perfectly straight spine that's free from tension. As a result of this, you should find your shoulders are relaxed and not slouched, nor should they be up by your ears.[4]

To maximise the Bespoken Technique of Posture for speaking, add the following steps:

- Rock gently forwards and backwards until you find your natural centre, where you're comfortable.
- Ever so slightly and ever so subtly, connect the balls of your feet with the ground. This may include a minute tilt, but very subtle and then breathe deeply as if you're drawing strength up through the floor and into your body and exhale slowly from your mouth.

What you should be experiencing now is a free full breath - whole chest breathing or intercostal diaphragmatic breathing if you like big words.

How does this posture feel right now? Perhaps a little unnatural?

I will help take this perfect posture into a seated and walking position so that you can embed it more easily. We don't generally spend a lot of time standing so it may feel unnatural to stand still for a long time. But if we practise it in a seated position and in our walking, it will become embedded.

People often ask me at this stage, 'what do I do with my hands?' My advice is to do what is called BBC hands, from the training at the British Broadcasting Corporation for decades: close your hands in front of you loosely one way or the other, whichever is comfortable for you, at roughly bellybutton height. Alternatively, hang your hands by your side. The danger with hands by your side is that if you're wearing a jacket, sometimes you can end up fidgeting with the edges. There's also the temptation to sneak your hands into your pockets, which is disempowering because these are your greatest tools of emphasis. So, hands by your side or folded nicely into BBC hands and from there you can gesture quite naturally.

Exercise 5b: Seated Posture

In order to make the standing posture easier to adopt, let's take it into sitting and walking. Get into your Bespoken Technique of Posture for standing – ankles, knees not locked, hips, shoulders, sternum, chin - perfect. Now, sit down.

Focusing on the upper part of your body for balance and strength,

Sit with your bum in the corner of your chair – between the seat and the back, line up your shoulders with your hips again, chin in line with your sternum, sternum lifted and hands either on the table in front of you, BBC hands, or resting on your thighs, but if possible, visible if you're behind a table, especially in an interview. And of course, use gesture as much as is natural for you; gesture adds emphasis to your speech.

Just a quick tip here from a Core Postural physiotherapist I've worked with. In everyday life, this is a strong posture that will maintain a back that's free from pain. If you're bending forward at your desk or in a meeting, don't bend from the shoulders, bend from the hips and keep your sternum lifted.

Exercise 5c: Walking Posture

Walk across the room.

What do you think you're led by? Which part of your body - your forehead, your nose, your chin, your shoulders, your chest, your hips, knees, feet? Have a go.

The way you walk communicates something about you and your confidence levels. The ideal walk – one that projects power and confidence - is to imagine that a string is attached to your sternum, leading you across the room. So that would be walking led by your chest.

Practise that a few times, at a moderate pace, and think about how you feel, knowing it will take time to become embedded if it's not what you do naturally. But realise that being led by a different part of your body is not only disempowering, but it sends a message to those who see you. A couple of examples: if you're led by your chin, it means that you have your chin slightly tilted and to your audience it could look somewhat arrogant. Same with the nose, as if there's a bad smell in the room! I worked with a very laid-back guy in the States who was led by his knees. 'Urgent' was not part of his vocabulary!

Be conscious of what you're communicating non-verbally and what it looks like to other people. Adopt what you can really own. But I can guarantee that being led by the chest is optimal for voice, eye contact and appearance. In terms of public speaking, it sets you up for the next stage I'll take you through. When you stand in it, you will sit in the Bespoken Technique of Posture far more naturally, and vice versa.

When this has become embedded, people will notice that you project more confidence - because that is the truth. When we're led by the upper part of our body, particularly the chest, we do project more confidence and we naturally lift our chin to just the right height because it's lined up with our sternum. People generally find it easier to place confidence in those projecting confidence and the speaker feeds off this confidence, which leads to them projecting even more… and so the virtuous circle of confidence continues.

Exercise 5d: Engaging your voice

Whilst standing in the Bespoken Technique of Posture count aloud from one to ten. Where were you looking and how did you sound?

Practise with this posture for when you are speaking in front of an audience or a camera.

- Find a point just above eye level on the back wall. This becomes your 'home' point. When you are on camera, you must make eye contact with the camera or your audience – whatever gives the perception that you are making eye contact.

- Count aloud from one to ten and imagine the numbers landing on that point.

Your home point must always be your returning point when you're not making eye contact. Obviously, you can't maintain eye contact with people all the time. If your default is to look down, how does it look to your audience? Ironically, you look a bit 'down', or depressed, but you're also closing off an important facial feature – your eyes! Are you familiar with the expression 'the eyes are the window of the soul'? You're disconnecting, disengaging from your audience, or are perceived as doing so. The second thing that is happening when looking down is that your voice drops somewhat. As a speaker, unless it's a device as part of your narrative (and even then, there are better ways to do it), you don't want a voice that sounds depressed in any way. It just gives you a negative demeanour so it's best to keep your face lifted so that your demeanour is more positive and open for your audience.

You may be questioning how long you should stay in this posture - for the whole of your speech? No - just as long as is necessary to engage your audience. You may of course move around, but that movement needs to be motivated. Don't just move aimlessly, don't do it because you're feeling uncomfortable or awkward, or it's your habit. Maintain a stable posture that projects power and confidence and then move when it's for a good reason or to make a point. Think about that and practise it.

Chapter 5
Opening the Breath System for
Whole Chest Breathing

You should now have support for your body in place: a body that's free from tension, and good posture that projects power and confidence, and you've started to become conscious of breathing that maximises the breath for speaking.

Before we continue, here are a few questions that matter.

What powers the voice?

… It's the breath.

And where is this breath made?

… It's produced in the lungs.

Therefore, it figures that if we want to make the most of our voice, we must make the most of our lung capacity so that we've got a breath that can produce the best possible voice. The negative reaction in the body that comes from speaking to a large audience or a camera can often manifest itself in shallow breathing, which leads to a shortness of breath and words become unclear, or ends of sentences get swallowed. It's important to maximise breath potential for speech.

Let's start by getting into our Bespoken Technique of Posture. Then we're going to consciously open the four areas of the breath system: front, sides, back and base, as seen in Fig. 4 below.

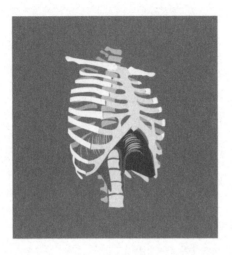

Fig 4

Exercise 6: Front stretch

Put your hands in front of you, straight out with palms together, then open them wide until they're in line with your body, creating a T-shape. As we open our arms out and wide, this is stretching the chest. Now, breathe deeply; in, through the nose and out through the mouth.

Repeat. Breathe in deeply, hands extended; in through the nose, imagine the air going down the throat, into the lungs, into the bronchi, into the bronchiole, filling up the lungs. And exhaling …

On the third breath, make sure that you're looking at that point above eye level we covered with posture. So, breathing in deeply and fully and slowly bringing the arms down as we exhale and, as you do, count to ten aloud – one, two, three, four, five, six, seven, eight, nine, ten. Smiling, imagine the breath sending the numbers to the spot above eye level. How does that feel? Tune into your body's response as you do each exercise. How does it sound?

Next, we're going to open up the sides of the breath system.

Exercise 7: Side Stretch

Just open your legs a little bit wider and bring one arm over your head in a shallow arc so that your fingertips are above your opposite shoulder. You should feel a stretch along the side of your now-stretched rib cage. Breathing in deeply, experiencing that breath along your side, and exhaling slowly. Now, bring your arm down and repeat on the other side. Breathing in. Place your opposite hand on your hip for balance if you wish. Stretching your hand above your head so it's in line with the opposite shoulder, breathing in and out. If possible, looking at that point above eye level or where the camera would be. And breathe as you return to an upright position.

Exercise 8: Back stretch

The largest opening in the breath system is in the back. This is one reason why you should avoid placing your hands behind your back when you're speaking. Apart from the fact that it will limit your ability to gesture, it also reduces your ability to utilise whole chest breathing.

Firstly, give yourself a hug from your Bespoken Technique of Posture position. Now, drop from the waist, as gently as you need to for your level of flexibility. Your hips are still going to be in line with your ankles, knees bent, but you're flopped over still hugging yourself and breathe in deeply. As you breathe, feel that breath going right into and down your back and, as you exhale, just drop your hands down so that you're completely limp from the waist up. Breathe deeply again; in and out. Once more, slowly in and slowly out again.

On the next exhale you're going to start coming up into a standing posture. But rise one vertebra at a time from the base of your spine up, slowly, on a count of about 16 – one, two, three, four, five, six, seven, eight – neck and shoulders should still be completely limp, nine, ten and bringing your shoulders, 11, 12, 13, 14 and your head up slowly and finally on 15 and 16. Ending in an upright posture, take one nice deep breath so that you can feel the benefit of this stretch.

The last place we need to work on here is the base of the breath system. This is where the diaphragm connects to the gut when we breathe a deep, connected breath. The gut is the emotional centre of the body so it's vital that our breath accesses that for tone colour and modulation. This gut connection won't surprise you if you've had a gut feeling or been nervous and had 'butterflies in your tummy'.

Research has shown that there are about 100 billion neurons in the human brain and about 500 million in the gut.[1] They are connected to the brain via one of the biggest nerves, the vagus, and this can be indirectly stimulated by deep breathing and meditation.[2] You've already done deep breathing all the way through these exercises.

The next two exercises ensure that gut connection is made as you prepare to speak. Then when you speak, your capacity for vocal variety through being in touch with your emotions is present.

Exercise 9: Connection 1

For the first exercise, you need a partner, a wall or a door. Place your hands against your partner's hands or against the surface, at about chest height. To judge the distance from the wall, play with a distance that allows you to bend your arms at the elbow slightly. Breathe in, and as you exhale, press in firmly, count aloud to ten and feel that connection in your diaphragm – one, two, three, four, five, six, seven, eight, nine, ten. With a partner, this might be more about resisting as they push.

Did you experience a gut connection or increased vocal strength in your voice? This sometimes takes time to experience, so work on it daily and seek to tune in to this. If you are a highly visual person, it may help to imagine a string connected to the centre of your diaphragm and running down each arm. As you apply pressure with a partner or a surface, imagine that string becoming taut and creating that connection and strength.

Exercise 10: Connection 2

The second is called the Kabuki. Patsy Rodenburg, my voice and speech guru, learnt it in Japan. It's a Japanese warrior and dancing exercise and it's excellent for achieving vocal connection with the gut.

Maintain the Bespoken Technique of Posture. Bending your knees, come down into a seated position as low as is comfortable for you, keeping your shoulders, hips and ankles lined up. This is not a squat. Imagine, if it helps, that there are giant skewers through your shoulders, hips and ankles and you are just sliding down them! A less gory image one of my clients has tried is to use the wall or a door jamb as a guide – just don't lean against them as the balance needs to come from within.

Find that point above eye level and breathing in deeply and slowly, place your fingertips just under the rib cage as you count aloud on the outgoing breath, one through to ten. Did you feel that connection? You should feel your voice connecting here, under your rib cage, as a little pulse. Come up slowly into a standing position.

If you're struggling to experience that connection, cough a little. The connection is far more subtle when you speak but it should help you realise it's there.

I suggest you keep practising both exercises until you find the one that's right for you. Then, if you so choose, drop the other one. Do both if you can; the point is to practise achieving that connection at the base of your breath system.

Having established this connection, the final exercise is about connecting your voice with your breath.

Exercise 11: Connection 3

Pretend that you're throwing a ball over arm. As you repeat it, think about when you inhale and at what exact point you begin exhaling.

We breathe in as we pull back our arm, and as we release, we exhale. Part of the momentum behind our throw is in our breath force.

It's the same when we speak. It's called 'speaking in the moment' and we do it naturally in normal conversation. It's important to carry this into public speaking, as the empowered connection with our words maximises our impact for engagement with our audience.

We're now going to repeat the throw, but we're going to 'throw' a word with our voice as we're throwing that imaginary ball. Choose one word, any word of your choice; I like 'yes' because it's short and crisp. Deliver that word with enthusiasm like you would release a ball … YES!

If we're anxious when we speak, we may begin exhaling before we start to speak. This is akin to throwing the ball when our arm is already halfway forward – all the momentum and half the power are gone. Some might even try to speak on an inhalation if they're nervous enough – that's the verbal equivalent of letting go of the ball when you're drawing your arm back. Both are ineffective and lacking in power. Remember – breathe in and speak, releasing words on the arc of the breath with full power and momentum.

This is the first time we've actively engaged speaking, as opposed to counting, in this series of exercises. It's vital that the support, breathing and connection are in place first. This is always going to be the case for speaking with power and confidence. These exercises should take about six minutes when you're used to practicing them. But we're not done yet!

Chapter 6
What About Facial Expression and Articulation?

The whole body left the face out - release!

There is an expression I learned from my teenagers which is not very polite but describes exactly an issue with the expressions on many faces we see around us today. It's commonly called a 'resting bitch face' (RBF) and is a face that looks cross when it is at rest, and it transcends gender, race and culture from what I've experienced.

Why do so many people refrain from smiling or even appear to frown? That's a big question but I can imagine a few answers. Life is often serious and as we grow to adulthood the responsibilities of living and learning and the concentration that takes can often show up on our faces. There are probably more reasons to have an unsmiling face than not, but the result is that we often carry a lot of unwanted, unnecessary tension in our faces. This will not serve us for public speaking. It is not engaging to look upon.

Two quick stories

A wonderful client who lives in the heart of Oxford city learned the value of a smile through these exercises. A couple of weeks later he reported that his dog walk had become a transformational experience! Apparently, in the past, the crowds parted as he approached with his innocuous labradoodle, but since he developed the natural ability to rest his face in a smile, many people smiled back at him as they passed by. As a frequent visitor to busy Oxford, I'm not sure I would lose the benefit of crowds parting, personally!

A fellow trainer experienced a trainee staring at him with a RBF through an entire day's delivery. It was quite off-putting and quite draining as it's easily perceived as disapproval or dissatisfaction. At the end of the day, the chap approached the trainer and expressed how much value he has gotten from the training. 'Well,' said the trainer, 'I wish you'd told your face because that was quite terrifying!'

If you have followed the exercises so far, you will have freed tension and learned the benefits of relaxing to provide support for the breath and voice. The Bespoken Technique of Posture gives you a body that demonstrates an openness to communication. Not only are you open to speaking but you are welcoming responses from your audience. Your face needs to follow through with this message.

This is one reason I'm going to spend some time focusing on the face and in particular the jaw. There is a second reason. In the next chapter we're going to look at the resonators, the places in the body where the voice gets bigger when it vibrates in the voice box. Two of these resonators are the mouth and open spaces in the skull such as the sinuses. However, if the face and jaw are carrying tension, commonly a clenched jaw, this will work against the voice reaching its full potential.

Jaw and tongue release

I call these group of exercises RELEASE, but first a little background to the problem.

As part of teenage angst, we may start carrying tension in our jaw. Some teenagers start mumbling, for others, it might mean a withdrawal from speaking. 'Grunting' is how some parents experiencing teenage communication describe it. But as part of the identity crisis many teenagers go through, their voice is affected

Sadly, if there's no intervention, we're going to take the problem, or at least a residual part of it, into adulthood. Interventions might include belonging to a school debating club, singing in a choir or doing drama. Today, more and more young people attend counselling so they have a safe space to work through issues, and this may help them retain or find their voice.

But in the majority of cases, many people develop a tight jaw. This affects articulation, vocal quality and creates facial tension that affects how we are seen by others and inhibits our facial expression. It can also lead to us carrying our voice in our throat and so we lack vocal power and connection, but it can also lead to speech that isn't articulate and a voice that isn't fully released.

Therefore, in order to maximise the use of the resonators, it's important to maximise the potential of the voice and create a better-quality sound, as well as ensuring our faces are free from tension.

These exercises also help maximise the potential of the mouth, where articulation happens.

Exercise 12a: Biting an apple

- Imagine that you are biting into a very large apple - opening your mouth as wide as possible and closing it on a bite. Repeat twice. You may hear a click in the jaw; that could be a sign of the tension you're releasing.

This exercise brings back fond memories of apple bobbing or biting into an apple hanging from the rafters on Halloween. You had to put your hands behind your back to avoid the temptation to cheat!

Exercise 12b: Tongue Stretch

The tongue is a very important tool in articulation so it's important to make sure that it's getting an occasional workout.

- Imagine you're licking an ice cream.
- Try to lick your nose, then stretch your tongue tip to your chin, your ear and your other ear. I call this exercise NSEW – north, south, east and west.
- Now wipe your mouth as it's sure to be quite wet!

Exercise 12c: Teeth brushing with tongue

- Imagine you're brushing your teeth with your tongue – all around the mouth, outside the teeth, top and bottom, inside, again - top and bottom, and finally, the ridge top and bottom.

Exercise 12d: The Yawn

No one fails on this next exercise; there's nothing quite like permission for a good yawn. As mentioned previously, it is the yawn that helps to lift and exercise the muscle where our soft palate lies.

Have a nice big yawn, breathing in through your nose, opening your mouth wide as you yawn. You can repeat if you like, but next time, try to yawn with your mouth closed. Breathe in and imagine you're suppressing a yawn in a very boring meeting. You should be aware of your soft palate lifting.

> **Yawn into old age**
>
> I had a client who was diagnosed with Parkinson's Disease a year into working together. It emerged from the exercises the Speech Therapist was doing with him that soft palate exercises are a good proactive exercise in preparation for old age. When we get older muscle fibres and connective tissue that make up the soft palate can become flabby or relaxed and that's where choking becomes a problem. Keeping that muscle strong and toned is therefore a very good idea.

Exercise 12e: Chewing Gum

The next exercise incorporates both the jaw and the tongue. If you are short of time when you're doing the whole exercise sequence, this is the one that you can do as a standalone because it encompasses exercising both the jaw and the tongue.

- Imagine you're chewing one piece of gum. Chew it all over your mouth.
- Repeat, adding an imaginary second piece, then a third.
- Imagine the fourth piece makes a ball of gum so big, you can't politely keep your mouth closed. Open your mouth as you're chewing. Make the rudest face and the widest mouth possible.

You should feel that you're exercising your tongue and all the muscles in the lower part of your face as you do this.

Exercise 12f: Facial Massage

The final exercise is about the whole face; you're going to give yourself a little facial massage.

- Starting with the hinges where the jaw meets the skull give yourself a nice rotational massage. I like to use the middle and index fingertips of both hands.
- Move across to your chin, meeting in the middle and come back out to the hinge.

- Now come across the cheek to the philtrum (under the nose) and back out again.
- Work your fingertips up into the temples and do some nice rotational movement there before coming across the cheekbones to the nose and back again.
- Next, across the forehead and back to the temples. You can tap instead of rotating, on any of the movements across an area, if you prefer. Play with what works best for you.
- Finally, stroke the whole face upwards with the hands, then down, leaving the jaw nice and loose. I end with an upward stroke so that it's easier to end on a smile.

We carry a lot of tension in our face of which we may be unaware, and these exercises should ensure our resting face is presenting a more open and pleasant countenance to others.

Those are the six release exercises which prepare us beautifully to move on to Resonance. Before we do that, let's address smiling.

And now smile!

If the eyes are the window to the soul, you could say the smile is the window to the heart. Now that we've released tension from the face, jaw and tongue, what is the best resting face to have for public speaking?

It has been said that you only get one chance to make a first impression. If our face is rather stern it will take people longer to engage with us and it's a shame to turn an audience off before we've started. Even if our subject matter is quite serious, nothing says, 'I'm glad to see you' or 'I'm pleased to be here' like a smile. A second advantage is that it releases endorphins and other happy chemicals, in the body.[1]

There is a third advantage to a smile: it makes the mouth bigger. There are in fact only two ways to make the mouth bigger: one is by opening the jaw more; the other is by lifting the soft palate. Refer to Fig. 5 and imagine a theatre is modelled on the mouth. Think of the tongue as the red velvet seats, the teeth the box seats on the side and the roof of your mouth the dome of the theatre. If you want more sound, you need to create more space for the sound to resonate. The one option is to open your mouth wider when you speak, and the second way is to lift the soft palate.

Exercise to find the soft palate:

- Place your tongue tip on the back of your upper teeth.
- Bring it back to the ridge behind your teeth (the alveolar ridge).
- Bring it back across the roof of your mouth to about halfway – you should be able to feel the hard palate as you do so.
- Behind this is the soft palate.

Lifting this will change the tone of the voice beautifully. If you follow the exercise below, you will hear the difference. Smiling when you speak is important, even just carrying a smile in your voice. But you can also achieve this through the yawn exercise above.

The Organs of Speech

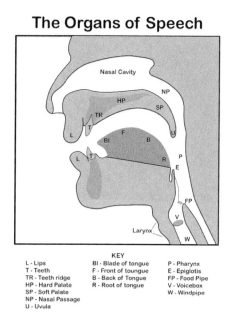

KEY		
L - Lips	Bl - Blade of tongue	P - Pharynx
T - Teeth	F - Front of toungue	E - Epiglotis
TR - Teeth ridge	B - Back of Tongue	FP - Food Pipe
HP - Hard Palate	R - Root of tongue	V - Voicebox
SP - Soft Palate		W - Windpipe
NP - Nasal Passage		
U - Uvula		

Fig. 5

Chapter 6

Smiling exercise

- Without smiling, say: 'Hello, my name is …; thank you for having me here.'
- Now smile and repeat those words. Can you hear the difference in your voice?

What does a smile say to other people? What does warmth in your voice convey? It also shows that you're comfortable to be there. Even if you're not quite comfortable yet, I believe in the principle of a virtuous circle. If you act like you're comfortable and confident, people will put their confidence in you and feel comfortable in your presence. When people are, you feel more comfortable and confident, and so on. Think about how other people make you feel when they smile at you in the audience. How does that make you feel? As the Good Book says, go and do likewise!

Chapter 7
How Can I Speak with A Rich, Full Voice?

Explaining resonance and its importance

Let's pause for a moment and consider where we're going on this breathtaking journey. The goal is to effectively engage and connect with an audience. I have outlined the transformational process from Chapter Five: relaxation, breathing, posture, expanding the breath system and connecting the breath with activating the voice. The previous chapter focused on releasing the facial and speech muscles to facilitate the best use of the voice. You now have and should be practising a series of regular exercises to embed this positive behaviour.

In this chapter, we're going to actively engage that wholly prepared body to release the voice.

Why does this matter you may ask. One of the most popular reasons people contact me is to improve their projection. I explain that this comes last in the process, because, if we can maximise the sound of the voice *in* the body and use the body as a whole instrument, projection will be effortless. It's like a double bass reverberating with rich sound from within the whole instrument and filling an auditorium as the bow connects correctly with the strings: you're not going to cause vocal strain when you're carrying the responsibility for vocal strength in the whole body. The strength is being carried from within; the bow simply releases it.

Good resonance maximises vocal strength. Resonance is defined in the glossary, but let me add two further definitions, 'a quality imparted to voiced sounds by vibration in anatomical resonating chambers or cavities', and 'a quality of richness or variety.'[1]

Speaking with a resonant voice can be equated to playing a piano with ten fingers rather than just playing the melody with one finger. You can produce a richer voice from a wider register and a voice with more timbre.

Activating the resonators

To produce a resonant voice, think about which chambers and cavities in the body could help produce vibration. If the voice can produce a sound akin to that of a bee buzzing in the voice box alone, according to an ENT (ear, nose and throat) Specialist, where do you think it's made bigger? Where does it vibrate?

There are five different places. The five resonators are the throat, mouth, chest, nose and sinuses - the open spaces in the head - and I always imagine that some of us have more open spaces than others! It's possible you are using some or all these already or perhaps, like many people, you're using only two or three. Checking that you're able to engage all of them and practising the next couple of exercises will ensure that you're maximising the potential of all the resonators.

Exercise 13a

For the first exercise, hum into all the resonators. Humming keeps the voice inside the body which facilitates vibration. The only place we can't hum with a 'mmm' sound is the nose. For that we'll use an 'ng' sound, as in 'sing'.

- Starting with the mouth, place your fingertips gently on your closed lips and take a relaxed, deep nasal breath. Hum so that your lips vibrate – 'mmm'. It should feel like a tickle. If you're struggling to experience the vibration, start with an open mouth instead, releasing the vowel sound 'aah' and then close your mouth into 'mmm'; this is easier for some[2].

- Send that hum down into your throat and feel the vibrations on your voice box, around the front and middle of your neck: 'mmm'. Feel the vibration with your fingertips. As a strong visual learner, I like to imagine a bee that I'm sending into these various resonators. If that helps you, use it; if it doesn't, ignore it.
- The next resonator is the chest. You may need to pitch your voice down for this and lower the note, but eventually you'll be able to do all of these on your natural middle note: 'mmm'. Feel the vibration by placing your flattened hand on your breastbone/sternum.
- Now bring the hum up into the nose. This is an 'ng' sound, as you need to close off your mouth. Feel that vibration on the bridge of your nose with your fingertips. Say 'sing' if it helps and extend the 'ng' until you feel the vibration.
- Next, hum into the top of your head, placing your fingertips across your scalp. You may need to pitch the note higher for this one: 'mmm'.

How was that? It may take practise before you can experience them all easily. As an extra reinforcement, you can do the following exercise.[3]

Exercise 13b

- Take a deep nasal breath and play with sending the hum to different resonators in no particular order, on one breath. Remember to keep your shoulders relaxed and use whole chest breathing.

Just to recap, ensuring you release your voice and access all five resonators internally will ensure that you have a full resonant voice.

Case study

Sadly, it is my experience that a significant number of people carry their voice in their throats. There are a couple of reason for this, but a common finding for me is that they've received criticism in their childhoods, about who they are or what they've said. It may be specifically regarding their singing or speaking voice. Those who do have difficulty with reclaiming the right to speak, to hold their voice in their mouth and release it out into the space they inhabit. Psychologically and often subconsciously, they don't feel like they have a right to speak. This might be you.

Some years ago, I coached a lovely Welsh man who was very softly spoken. He was extremely intelligent and an expert in his field. My details had been passed on to him because he was very shy. He eventually came to me when he was contemplating going for interviews. We were making progress, but a breakthrough came when I made a casual remark while coaching him through the resonance exercises. As I talked about pitch and releasing the voice, I said light-heartedly, 'Of course this is no problem for you: Welsh people sing beautifully.'

'Not for me,' he replied, 'A teacher in primary school asked me if I could mouth the words when I sang in a choir.'

POW!

Between him expressing these words, possibly for the first time ever, and the expression on my face at hearing them, he realised how the words had impacted him. Perhaps she was more focused on getting praise for the choir's performance than on the self-esteem of a young boy. She probably spoke the words aloud before a classroom full of children. I don't know if anyone sniggered or teased. It didn't matter. A significant person in his life had criticised him at a tender age and it had affected his voice ever since.

Does that resonate with you? It could be a parent, a sibling, a friend or even an enemy. Naming it for what it was may help you bring your voice forward. Telling someone about it may help. But bring it out into the light and see it for what it is. Remember, 'there is no such thing as a bad voice, only a voice with blocks in it.'[3]

Allow the truth that you have a right to speak and a right to be heard, replace the limiting belief that was planted back then.

Playing a chord with our body and letting it out

The next step is to bring all that sound together into one note and to release it out through the mouth.

Exercise 14

Extending the analogy I used earlier, imagine you've got five bees, one in each resonator. You're going to hum to make them all buzz on one note.

- In your Bespoken Technique of Posture, as always, relax your shoulders and place your fingertips on the top of your head and on your sternum, so that you can experience your voice resonating from the highest to the lowest part of your resonance system.
- On a deep exhaling breath, hum for about five seconds or until you feel the vibrations in both places.
- Opening your mouth wide and relaxing your jaw fully, release the 'mmm' into 'aah'. We choose 'aah' as it's the most open vowel sound. Extend that release on 'aah' until you feel the breath support go.

Repeat, and as soon as you feel the breath support go, stop because the last thing you want is to strain your breath system.

And those are your resonance exercises, discovered, explored and employed.

Chapter 8

How Do I Make Sure People Hear Me?

Introducing Breath Control

The next layer in the foundation work is breath control. With support and breathing now in place, and breath connected to a voice that is released and resonant, breath control can be effortless. Do you have control over your breath when engaging your voice? It's important to check that our breath can support the phrase or sentence we wish to speak.

Why else does it matter? If you have heard anyone being complimented for command of their speech, breath control will be one reason. I believe this is a compliment, not just of their vocabulary but also of their ability to control delivery of the spoken word. The words are created by the voice, which in turn is powered by the breath. Therefore, good breath control is vital: knowing your breath capacity, knowing how best to use it, and knowing its limitations. Good breath control gives confidence to speak with ease.

And the flip side? Have you noticed that sometimes people lose a word or two at the end of their sentences, or they seem to fade out towards the end of what they're saying? The result is that you lose the sense of the sentence, it no longer makes sense. In my experience, I say "pardon?" only to have them do the same again. This is largely due to lack of good breath control.

Even if we normally seem to manage decent breath control, we may find it challenging when public speaking. What I like to call 'the adrenaline effect' which may mean that we have less breath force as shortness of breath may impact our capacity. It's important to build up a good breath system and good breath control so that we can feel confident in delivering what we need to say competently, confidently and creating a positive experience for our audience.

Before you undertake the following two exercises, allow me to explain briefly why we're using the letters 's' and 'z' to do them. Different words make varying demands on our voice because of the formation of particular sounds. If you place your fingertips on your voice box and hiss 'sss' you will notice that there is no vibration. This is because the sound is formed entirely at the front of the mouth. With 'z' the same organs of speech are used but this time, when you make the 'zzz' sound you can feel the vibrations on your voice box. This is because that sound is created in the throat. By using both sounds we ensure that both the voiced 'z' and unvoiced 's' are employed in breath control.

Vocal 1: Exercise 15a

- Begin with the Bespoken Technique of Posture as always.
- Breathe in deeply through the nose and into the whole chest.
- Exhale on a count of 15 making an s-sound. It sounds like a hiss. Use your fingers to count out the seconds, or a timer if you wish. Remember to keep facing forward and look at eye-level or just above to maximise your posture.
- Relax and repeat for a count of 20. You could try to build up to 35 in increments of five but stop as soon as you feel the breath support going. Speaking without breath support is never going to sound good so there's no point practising it!

With practise, you will achieve 35 seconds if you don't have the capacity to accomplish it first time around. I have had both a bassoon, a clarinet player and a singer as clients, and all of them had great lung capacity due to the breath they had built up through practising with their instruments. Some professional actors repeat an exhalation on these sounds for 35 seconds seven times consecutively for the vocal demands of stage acting, but I believe 25-30 seconds is adequate for most business presentations.[1]

TWO TOP TIPS:

If you are struggling to reach the longer counts, remember it's not about volume or power, it's about sustaining your breath. Try again with a softer volume, less power and just aim to get to the 'finish line'.

It's often a childhood habit to lift our shoulders when we're making a big effort to breathe in. Relax your shoulders and ensure your breath is coming from your whole lungs and connected to your diaphragm and your emotional centre in your gut, as you've learned above.

Vocal 1: Exercise 15b

- Repeat the above exercise, but use the *z*-sound, a buzzing rather than a hissing.

Introducing projection

One of the leading reasons people reach out to work with me, is projection. They want to learn to project their voices. "I want to be heard," they say, or a facsimile thereof. And I will tell you what I tell them: once you learn to use your whole body to speak, projection will be effortless. This is the final exercise in the foundational work.

'If you can breathe a space, you own it. After that, everyone is coming into your space' - Patsy Rodenburg.

I find that so empowering.

Imagine believing that as you sit before an interview panel. Imagine believing that in front of an auditorium full of people. Believing this increases confidence and a sense of ownership of the space we're in, which is important if we want to project power, clarity and confidence to our audience.

It's worth noting at this point that projection is different to volume. I know from being at school and from working with teachers in schools, that they often tell students to 'speak up' and 'speak louder' when they can't be heard. Many people mistake volume with projection.

Projection is about our voice reaching our audience, about us sending our voice to their ears. It's about the strength of the voice and its power. Tone volume is about modulation, how loudly or softly we speak depending on the requirements of the text and our use of vocal variety. I'll go into volume in more detail in Chapter 14, but suffice to say, that if you use volume instead of projection to be heard, you may be shouting. Your audience may feel they're being shouted at which is never a good thing, and if this is happening, you not only switch your audience off, but reduce the impact of your ability to use other techniques of modulation. So, while there may be an increase in volume as you go through these exercises, it won't be significant, and the focus is on projecting or sending your voice forward. If you need to be loud to be heard, it's time to use a megaphone or a microphone, depending on the context. Working with amplification tools is covered elsewhere.

Vocal 2: Exercise 16

- Stand well back with the room in front of you; the larger the room you can practise in the better.
- Place your hand in front of you, an elbow's length from your face.
- Adopting the Bespoken Technique of Posture, breathe deeply and exhale, so that your breath reaches your palm. For this exercise, I like to visualise a little red laser dot that I'm breathing in through my nose, down my throat into my lungs, touching my diaphragm and returning back out so that it lands on my hand.
- Extend your arm fully and slightly above eye level. Repeat the exercise breathing in through the nose and out through the

mouth, remembering to breathe, not blow. Next, face a wall about a metre or three feet away and repeat the exercise; breathing in, and out.

- Next, look towards the furthest corner of the room and repeat, breathing in and out so that you imagine your breath landing back in the corner of the room.
- Now, think of your favourite colour. Imagine a red glow that fills the room, like the laser dot colour. Breathe it in deeply and slowly as you look around the room, inhaling that colour. Then imagine breathing out your favourite colour so that its glow fills the room.
- Repeat the exercise but with the word 'yes' or a similar short, crisp word of your choice. Start with your hand at elbow's length. Speak 'yes' to this distance as if to a person close to you in a room, then at arm's length, which could be a person in a conversation circle, repeat for one metre away (similar to the distance of six people around a meeting room table), then to the furthest corner and finally to the whole room. You may wish to repeat the word or speak a short sentence as you look around the room.

I would encourage you to make every effort to visit a venue before you speak there and do this exercise while it's unoccupied. If you've got someone escorting you, just let them know you're checking out the acoustics! The benefit is enormous as the space becomes demystified as you breathe it. I have found this to be true and my clients have found it very empowering.

Chapter 9
A Foundation for a Lifetime of Speaking

I'm quite partial to confessions, so let me make one here. In the exams I studied to qualify as a Speech and Drama Teacher, twenty-five per cent of the marks in both written papers were about voice production and the physiology of breath, voice and speech. I hated it, possibly because when I was a teenager, I'd had uninspiring science teachers in my convent school. But because the pass mark in all these Trinity College London diploma exams was seventy per cent, I had to knuckle down and seek to come to grips with it all. In the Licentiate practical exam, I even had to teach the examiner an aspect of this. For my sins, I had John Cheeseman, the then Chief Examiner!

Ironically, as I delivered lessons in my various studios over the following 16 years, I realised that voice production was the most fundamental skill I taught my students. Every lesson began with some breathing or relaxation exercise, something that helped engage their body and voice before they sought to act, to present, to engage. I grew to love it as I saw how important it was in developing ability and confidence in students. The pause to relax, deep breathing and entering the space, also helps students and clients to leave the world they inhabit outside the room and become present in the time and space they set aside for an hour.

Chapter 9

When I made the decision to focus on businesses and corporates, this priority remained. There are many people who can help with 'above the waterline' presentation skills and practitioners who can help with psychological techniques for confidence. My experience has been that if people are equipped with the skills and exercises you've been given from Chapter 4 to 8, the 'below the waterline' techniques, they have the toolbox within themselves to do the job with confidence, knowing they have the basic tools they can draw on in any given situation. Yes, there is more to add, but the foundational exercises are an essential framework that you can depend on as you move forward, invisible, like internal scaffolding!

The whole 'Rondo Sequence' and how to embed it into practise

Below, you will find a summary of the sixteen exercises contained in the last five chapters. I've put them into a sequence so that you can practise them daily, or on alternate days, until they are embedded in your muscle memory. Thereafter, use them prior to practising a presentation, interview, or speech and in advance of delivering it. If you wish, find a piece of music you love, one that inspires you and use this as your backing track. Think of it as your 'fight song'. The music I practise it to isn't exactly a fight song, but I call the set of exercises 'The Rondo Sequence' because I've always played Rondo Veneziano's 'Visioni di Venezia'[1] for myself or with classes. If I'm a later speaker in the morning or afternoon, I need only play the music in my head, along with a body check exercise, to be inspired and ready to speak.

I will add this as an appendix too so that you can copy or print out this sequence. You may wish to make a laminate to keep in the room where you practise. Make a few copies if you wish and carry one in your kit bag so you never forget it for a public speaking opportunity.

The content of each exercise is condensed, so simply refer to the relevant chapter if you forget the detail or the motivation for doing it. Where I've written ten, you should count aloud to ten on the outgoing breath. Counting aloud is not necessary on other exercises. The sixteen exercises take 12 to 15 minutes to do properly from start to finish. Remember to smile and enjoy!

I have included two versions; the second is for wheelchair users or those with mobility issues and is based on client work. In the second, (PA) indicates where assistance may be required.

Rondo Sequence

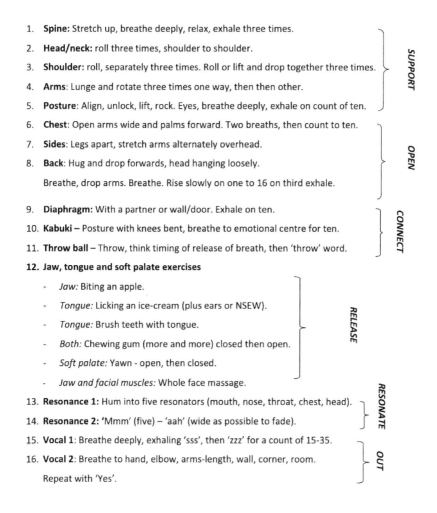

1. **Spine:** Stretch up, breathe deeply, relax, exhale three times.
2. **Head/neck:** roll three times, shoulder to shoulder.
3. **Shoulder:** roll, separately three times. Roll or lift and drop together three times.
4. **Arms**: Lunge and rotate three times one way, then then other.
5. **Posture:** Align, unlock, lift, rock. Eyes, breathe deeply, exhale on count of ten.

   SUPPORT

6. **Chest**: Open arms wide and palms forward. Two breaths, then count to ten.
7. **Sides:** Legs apart, stretch arms alternately overhead.
8. **Back:** Hug and drop forwards, head hanging loosely.

   Breathe, drop arms. Breathe. Rise slowly on one to 16 on third exhale.

   OPEN

9. **Diaphragm:** With a partner or wall/door. Exhale on ten.
10. **Kabuki –** Posture with knees bent, breathe to emotional centre for ten.
11. **Throw ball –** Throw, think timing of release of breath, then 'throw' word.

    CONNECT

12. **Jaw, tongue and soft palate exercises**

    - *Jaw:* Biting an apple.
    - *Tongue:* Licking an ice-cream (plus ears or NSEW).
    - *Tongue:* Brush teeth with tongue.
    - *Both:* Chewing gum (more and more) closed then open.
    - *Soft palate:* Yawn - open, then closed.
    - *Jaw and facial muscles:* Whole face massage.

    RELEASE

13. **Resonance 1:** Hum into five resonators (mouth, nose, throat, chest, head).
14. **Resonance 2:** 'Mmm' (five) – 'aah' (wide as possible to fade).

    RESONATE

15. **Vocal 1**: Breathe deeply, exhaling 'sss', then 'zzz' for a count of 15-35.
16. **Vocal 2**: Breathe to hand, elbow, arms-length, wall, corner, room.

    Repeat with 'Yes'.

    OUT

Remember from the detailed exercises that whenever ten is mentioned, this means counting aloud to ten on the outgoing breath. Do this 'in the moment' as learnt from exercise 11.

Chapter 9

Seated Rondo Sequence

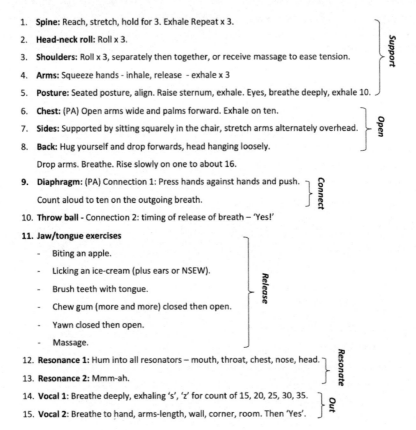

1. **Spine:** Reach, stretch, hold for 3. Exhale Repeat x 3.
2. **Head-neck roll:** Roll x 3.
3. **Shoulders:** Roll x 3, separately then together, or receive massage to ease tension.
4. **Arms:** Squeeze hands - inhale, release - exhale x 3
5. **Posture:** Seated posture, align. Raise sternum, exhale. Eyes, breathe deeply, exhale 10.

   Support

6. **Chest:** (PA) Open arms wide and palms forward. Exhale on ten.
7. **Sides:** Supported by sitting squarely in the chair, stretch arms alternately overhead.
8. **Back:** Hug yourself and drop forwards, head hanging loosely.

   Open

   Drop arms. Breathe. Rise slowly on one to about 16.
9. **Diaphragm:** (PA) Connection 1: Press hands against hands and push.

   Count aloud to ten on the outgoing breath.

   Connect

10. **Throw ball -** Connection 2: timing of release of breath – 'Yes!'
11. **Jaw/tongue exercises**
    - Biting an apple.
    - Licking an ice-cream (plus ears or NSEW).
    - Brush teeth with tongue.
    - Chew gum (more and more) closed then open.
    - Yawn closed then open.
    - Massage.

    Release

12. **Resonance 1:** Hum into all resonators – mouth, throat, chest, nose, head.
13. **Resonance 2:** Mmm-ah.

    Resonate

14. **Vocal 1:** Breathe deeply, exhaling 's', 'z' for count of 15, 20, 25, 30, 35.
15. **Vocal 2:** Breathe to hand, arms-length, wall, corner, room. Then 'Yes'.

    Out

The wheelchair-based client for whom I modified these exercises used a PA. Depending on your limitations and the assistance you have, you may be able to do more or less of the standing Rondo Sequence. As my client was an expert and advisor on EDI (equality, diversity and inclusion), we sought to make them as inclusive as possible.

Remember from the detailed exercises that whenever ten is mentioned, this means counting aloud to ten on the outgoing breath. Do this 'in the moment' as learnt from exercise 11.

Some shortcuts

I recognise that we all have busy lives so here are some shortcuts or variations for when you feel the exercises are embedded, that they've 'become you'. This reduces the sequence, to about 12 minutes.

You could print these shortcuts out and leave copies in your bathroom or bedroom so you can do them as part of your night-time or morning routine, e.g., release exercises when putting on day or night cream.

Unless otherwise stated, do the full exercise as summarised above. These shortcuts don't mean compromise or rush; they simply reduce the total time. I've underlined what is cut short for easy reference:

Step 3 – Shoulders: Just roll the shoulders forwards three times and then back three times. Variation: Lift your shoulders to your ears and tense three times on your nasal inhalation, then drop them on the exhalation. Or skip rolling one shoulder at a time and just roll the shoulders forward and back together.

Step 5 – Standing posture: It's important that the process is embedded before you do this exercise and have no spinal issues. Simply look ahead, jump and land. You'll find that you land in perfect posture – feet naturally two fists apart, ankles, shoulders and hips aligned, chin aligned with a slightly raised sternum and hands by your side. Remember I said that prior to age five, our posture is pretty much perfect? This proves it, I think!

Step 6 – Chest: Hold arms out to the side pushing back past the shoulder line to open the chest. for one breath and then count aloud to 10 whilst lowering them.

Step 8 – Back: From bent over position, exhale for one breath, start coming up on second exhale.

Step 10 or 11 – Connection: Do either Diaphragm or Kabuki, whichever you prefer, not both.

Step 12 – Jaw/tongue: Either do one jaw and one tongue exercise, or just do the Chewing Gum exercise as this engages both the jaw and the tongue.

Chapter 9

Step 15 – Breath control: Alternate exhaling on *'sss'* for 15 seconds, *'zzz'* for 20, *'sss'* for 25 seconds and so on, until you reach 35 seconds. Or start with *'zzz'* on 15 and alternate again with *'sss'*. Note that a count to 25 or 30 is adequate for most public speaking requirements.

SECTION THREE
What Comes Next?

Chapter 10
Introduction

Having read and understood the 'why' behind the exercises in the previous section, you should now have the foundation in place for effective spoken communication. You are ready to take your speaking to the next level.

Let's consider what we have done in rediscovering our innate ability to use our body and voice to communicate. It's almost akin to finding an old musical instrument in the attic that we've dusted off and cleaned up. The next step is to start playing it. It contains all the notes, tune and music that it was designed to play; it just needs you to bring them alive.

That is where you are now. Depending on the role-modelling and lessons with which you grew up, you have learned much of what you already need. But as with any learning, you've had a mixture of good and bad teachers, and this is what you've learned to emulate. Even if you've had very good role models communicating around you for everyday conversation, it's usual that when people are put in the spotlight to speak, much of the good practise that comes naturally, evaporates as nerves take over. Even if you can reframe that as excitement and use the breathing skills you've now learned, there is a potential that you could do better, be more engaging and connect with your audience more.

That is what this section is about. The word 'modulate' means to vary or change and is used with regard to sound. Vocal modulation for speaking is about varying your voice to maximise the potential of engaging with an audience. It's all very well for a foghorn or a church bell to sound with one regular note; it's even helpful as it alerts us to an approaching boat or upcoming service. But applied to the human voice, to speak without variety creates monotony and is, quite frankly, boring. In my ideal world, it would be a crime to subject an audience to a boring speaker – off with their heads!

I will take you through six aspects of modulation in this chapter. Which six and why six, you may ask? I studied these as part of my qualifications, and they've served my clients well over the years. I've not seen anything worth adding or taking away.

We'll also cover articulation, which helps with the clarity and crispness of speech. It matters because how well we shape and deliver our words affects the audience's experience and the ability to understand us. A few straightforward articulation exercises provide the potential, when practised, to elevate our speech and ensure that we are easily understood by our audiences.

The new millennium has made the term 'global village' a reality and, although English is currently the third most spoken language (after Mandarin and Spanish), it can be heard in a wide variety of accents. Accents are part of our personality and identity but if we wish to be understood by a global audience, we need to ensure that our accent is not a barrier to communication. Having considered and exercised skills of modulation and articulation, we'll examine what else we can do to ensure our accent plays an effective role in our spoken communication.

But we'll start with The Resonance Scale. This is something that touches on both modulation and articulation and because it's neither and both, it's a good place to begin. I've also written a little about reading aloud as this will be a valuable way to practise and embed your modulation technique.

The Resonance Scale

The Resonance Scale is a wonderful tool to understand and appreciate our voice's natural variations in pitch and how our mouth assumes different, distinctive shapes to form various vowel sounds. Playing with the Resonance Scale helps with vocal pitch and articulation. But remember that the aim is to engage an audience and to make it easier for them to connect with us. Vocal variety and good articulation facilitate this happening with ease.

As a result of practising this scale and speaking the sentence which follows, you will become aware that your voice has the potential to naturally vary in pitch if you're articulating the vocal sounds correctly. If you tend to speak in a monotone, it will help you discover the potential for pitch variation quite naturally. As an articulation exercise, you will learn to appreciate the subtlety of vowel sounds and how clarity of speech helps to avoid misunderstanding.

You should know by now that I like to ask questions to get your curiosity engaged. Here are a couple for you:

How many notes do you think the human voice can pitch when speaking?

How many notes do you think the average person hits in everyday speech?

We can hit up to 14 notes when we speak although the average English-speaker only hits about four![1] Now this could explain one of many reasons why only a small percentage of people stand out as good orators. I remember a Director's Workshop with Deon Opperman, founder of the South African film school, saying that it's the job of an actor to keep the audience awake. Think about it - comfortable seats in a dark theatre, often after a sumptuous meal out. The most natural thing for a body to do is fall asleep! The same could be said of some meetings or presentations. A boring voice can have a soporific effect, second to none.

Resonance Scale Exercise

Look at the words below:

HOOT
HOOK
HOE
HAWK
HOCK
HARD
HUT
HIRT
HEARD
HAD
HEAD
HAY
HID
HEED

The vowel sounds form a scale which require us to pitch our voice differently for each sound. If you 'speak' them with your mouth closed, you should hear that they each hit a subtly different note. If you were to play these notes with an instrument you would find that they are a semitone apart. For instance, with my vocal pitch, my first note on HOOT is' A' and each word descends by a semi-tone until I reach 'B' flat.

Articulate them aloud and experience the subtle differences between them. What else do you notice?

Take a mirror and repeat them, looking at your mouth for each utterance. What did you notice?

What you should observe is how the vowel sounds demand the mouth to assume different, distinctive shapes, getting bigger and wider as you descend the scale. If you like, just speak the vowel sounds which I've underlined above.

Finally, this sentence has all the above vowel sounds in the correct order and makes a great little articulation exercise. It's even better if you take time to over-emphasize each word.

Who would know aught of art must first learn and then take his ease

When to use this exercise:

I will often speak the Resonance Scale at the end of the Rondo Sequence. In fact, you could happily speak it, or the sentence above, as the final step in Exercise 15 – Projection, instead of speaking 'yes' to the entire room.

A word about reading aloud

The best way to progress your modulation skills is to practise reading aloud every day. Even just two minutes a day has several benefits. Firstly, reading aloud fires different neurons in your brain than reading in your head. They are the same neurons in the language centre of the brain that fire when you do public speaking, so it's a good idea to exercise them! As the experience becomes familiar, public speaking will begin to feel more natural.[2] Secondly, reading aloud is an ideal outlet to practise your modulation skills, especially if you have access to children's storybooks. Thirdly, it will help you get used to speaking out without expecting a response, as is the case when we present. You need to become used to this as it's one of the awkward obstacles that make people feel vulnerable. I want you to get used to the sound of your own voice in a space without interruption.

I've included material in this section for you to read when practising each component, but you'll be more motivated if you read material that you find personally interesting. I maintain I would have stuck at piano lessons for longer if I had enjoyed the pieces I was playing as a child. So, please feel free to read what you love. However, if I give you the criteria which I used to choose this material, I suggest you do the same when choosing your own. I recognise that most of you are possibly in careers where you are required to read non-fiction every day. Much of it is not designed to be read aloud and won't provide much inspiration for great modulation. However, if you use fiction while you're developing your skills, you can easily transfer these skills to your non-fiction material when necessary.

The criteria I recommend for choosing reading material:

- Fiction.
- It's well written. Classics or best sellers are safe bets. See the text box regarding Charles Dickens as an example.
- It reads well and easily aloud; it flows. Storybooks, especially traditional ones, fit this criterion as they were recorded from an oral tradition.
- It contains varied sentence lengths.
- It has some challenging words.
- If it's fun to read, that's a bonus!
- Most importantly – it's not on your phone. The size of the print and the length of the lines will not serve you well in developing speech flow.

3

The writings of Charles Dickens are marvellous to practise reading aloud. His books were originally published in serialised form in magazines in Victorian England where reading skills were not widespread. People would gather to listen to his stories in parlours. Dickens himself loved to perform public readings, so I imagine he wrote with a speaker reading it in mind. A criticism of Dickens is that he's too detailed. But he writes about people with great humour and insight and about England, London in particular, with a great social conscience. If you remember that his work predates television and widely available photography, you might appreciate how he wove wonderful stories and painted detailed word pictures of people and places. I find The Pickwick Papers, his first novel, particularly satirical.

Here are some guidelines for reading aloud so that you can make the most of it. It's written with reading to an audience in mind, so use your discretion when you're doing your two minutes reading aloud daily exercise. For several years, I've been a volunteer reader for a talking newspaper for the visually impaired and am surprised at how many people believe they can do it well without these considerations:

- Scan the passage for any difficult words.
- Scan it for punctuation.
- Audibility: Make sure that those at the back of the room can hear you.
- Analysis: Understanding the whole of what you are reading as well as each idea in the passage.
- Centring: Pick out the most important idea and make it stand out from other ideas in the phrase or sentence.
- Read it once to experience the shape of the word and phrases in your mouth.
- Now read it aloud for pleasure.

That will do for now. Shall we continue?

Chapter 11

How Do I Keep People Awake When I Speak!?

Vocal variety, or modulation, is a wonderful way our voices are designed to engage and connect with an audience so that they want to listen and hear what we have to say.

To get you thinking about modulation, an area of voice production, let's look at a couple of definitions, examples and synonyms given for the word 'modulate': [1]

> 1. exert a modifying or controlling influence on, e.g., "the state attempts to modulate private business's cash flow".

Similar: regulate, adjust, set, attune, balance, harmonize, temper, modify, moderate.

> 2. vary the strength, tone, or pitch of (one's voice), e.g., "we all modulate our voice by hearing it".

Similar: adjust, change the tone of, vary, inflect

I like the first definition because we can exert a modifying or controlling influence on our voices. We have that ability and once we know how, we can do it very well. We can also learn from others who do it. If you've ever heard Judi Dench being interviewed, she's a master of the art. Stephen Fry is an admirable male equivalent. And those synonyms under both definitions should inspire you to do the same.

The second definition is more conventional when used about music and voice. The six aspects of modulation can easily be remembered as three Ps and TIE: pitch, pace, pause, tone, inflection and emphasis. Let's explore them one by one.

Modulation pitch

Without going into unnecessary detail, pitch is how high or low we speak. The sound is created in our voice box or mouth and resonates in our body. Our middle pitch settles post-puberty and is influenced by our physical size. To use extreme examples from the animal kingdom, mice have a high-pitched squeak and elephants have a deep, resonant trumpet. Even within a dog breed, we can hear that a Yorkshire Terrier has a higher pitch than a Great Dane.

In humans, pitch is influenced by our sex as well as physical size. On average, the female voice has a range an octave higher than the male voice but there are broad ranges of voices for both sexes, influenced by the size and thickness of their vocal cords. Larger humans generally have deeper voices than smaller ones. If you think of these as default setting, you can be confident that increasing your pitch range and adjusting your moderate pitch, should you wish to, is within your influence.

Studies have found that people respond more positively to lower, more resonant voices.[2] They are experienced as more comforting and reassuring. This makes sense if you think of the voice used for putting a baby to sleep compared to a distressed voice. Tension in our body will cause our pitch to rise unnecessarily, which is why I included exercises to release tension in Chapter 7. Tension should not be an obstacle to public speaking if you've been practising these and the breathing exercises.

We change our pitch based on what we're thinking and feeling. What thoughts and feelings would normally raise or lower the pitch of your voice? Perhaps pause for a moment and have a think.

We communicate our thinking and feeling to others in our voices. Therefore, it's important that we understand what our voice is communicating and remove the barriers that might interfere with that communication. This facilitates the audience responding in the way you intended your spoken words to be received.

Thoughtful, measured responses are normally communicated in a more moderate pitch; impulsive, hasty speech is often communicated in a raised pitch. Fear and excitement tend to raise our pitch, while sadness, peace or solemnity tend to lower it. When we experience these emotions, it creates a physical reaction which tightens or relaxes our vocal cords. Why am I asking you to think about this? When we've rehearsed a presentation or response, we often lose that pitch variety in our voice. It's also possible we're not using a variety of pitch to communicate our thoughts or feelings in a less natural public speaking environment.

Have a read of this passage, then read it aloud to practise pitch variety. I've provided two copies, a clean one for you to use and mark if you wish. The second follows the section on pace, for reasons which will become clear.

Exercise for pitch

An extract from Lord of the Flies by William Golding.[3]

"'Listen. Listen for a long time."

Quite clearly and emphatically, and only a yard or so away from the back of the shelter, a stick cracked. The blood roared again in Ralph's ears, confused images chased each other through his mind. A composite of these things was prowling round the shelters. He could feel Piggy's head against his shoulder and the convulsive grip of a hand.

Chapter 11

"Ralph! Ralph!"
"Shut up and listen."
Desperately, Ralph prayed that the beast would prefer littluns.
A voice whispered horribly outside.
"Piggy–Piggy –"
"It's come!" gasped Piggy. "It's real!"
He clung to Ralph and reached to get his breath.
"Piggy, come outside. I want you Piggy."
Ralph's mouth was against Piggy's ear.
"Don't say anything."
"Piggy – where are you, Piggy?"
Something brushed against the back of the shelter. Piggy kept
*   still for a moment, then he had his asthma. He arched his*
*   back and crashed among the leaves with his legs. Ralph*
*   rolled away from him.'*

Modulation pace

Vocal pace is how quickly or slowly we speak. Every one of us has a moderate pace which will be influenced by our cultural and family norms; it's learned. But within a family, there will also be variations. Pitch and pace go together to some extent: when we're excited or agitated, our pace quickens as our pitch rises. Conversely, when we're relaxed, sad or thoughtful, our pace tends to slow and our pitch drops.

It's important to have control of pace for a few reasons. If we're agitated or nervous about public speaking, we will give this away if we speak quickly and this won't communicate power and confidence. It may also affect our clarity. Even if we are a naturally fast speaker, we may give the impression that we're nervous if that's what the listener associates with nervousness, and this will not instil confidence in our audience. But most importantly, it's vital to speak at a pace that allows our listener to process what we're saying. Otherwise, they will lose out on content and may eventually stop listening as they lose the thread of what we're saying.

Sound travels in waves; remember that from your school science? Now imagine if it travels from the ear to the brain of the listener at the rate by which they can process the information. I imagine a veritable traffic jam of sound waves building up outside the ear of my listener if I'm bombarding them with words they can't process! It doesn't sound like a pleasant listening experience, does it?

It's also true that if you can moderate your pace, you will have a wider variety of places to go vocally when you want to speed up to convey, say enthusiasm, or slow down to convey a weightier point. And variety is key for sustained engagement.

You may hear different words instead of pace, such as rate and speed. You may well wonder if they mean different things. Rate is simply the number of words a person speaks per minute. Speed considers how quickly a person speaks. So, they're interchangeable to some extent but I believe 'pace' is a broader term.

In order to engage with learning about pace, look at the *Lord of the Flies* passage above and decide what you would do to vary the pace as well as the pitch. Record your voice and play it back, listening without looking at the passage, and simply experience the pleasure of being engaged by the delivery. [4] You might be surprised to find that you naturally adjusted your pace to match your pitch. I've made notes in the passage below for ideas of what I might do. Remembering that, as the audience comes first, I would make a reading more or less dramatic depending on who is listening and the occasion. If I have a variety of age groups in the audience, I always adjust for the youngest. Older people were once young, and surely everyone loves a story well told!

Exercise for pitch and pace

An extract from *Lord of the Flies* by William Golding *[I will introduce this in a moderate pitch and pace to convey neutrality].*

"Listen. Listen for a long time." *[I speak Ralph's voice, in a lower pitch because I'm a female speaking a male voice, even though his voice may not have broken yet, to contrast with my own voice and Piggy's. I would drop my pitch, and indeed volume, if I was asking someone to listen. Because they are short sentences, I will speak them quite slowly. A good author uses sentence length to communicate pace to us.]*

Chapter 11

Quite clearly and emphatically, and only a yard or so away from the back of the shelter, a stick cracked. *[I will pick up the pitch and pace for this sentence, not only because it's quite long but because this paragraph builds a sense of urgency, drama, and some panic].*

The blood roared again in Ralph's ears, confused images chased each other through his mind. *[I will build the pace a little more and my pitch will rise].*

A composite of these things was prowling round the shelters. He could feel Piggy's head against his shoulder and the convulsive grip of a hand. *[I will slow down and lower my pitch slightly for each of these two sentences, partly because I want to communicate a little menace and dread, partially because the next two words require a high pitch and slightly hysterical faster pace].*

"Ralph! Ralph!" *[I will quicken my pace and use a higher pitch]*

"Shut up and listen." *[Ralph's pitch is lower and slower because he's trying to calm Piggy].*

Desperately, Ralph prayed that the beast would prefer littluns. *[Back to moderate, narrative pitch and pace].*

A voice whispered horribly outside.

"Piggy – Piggy – " *[This is the group of children trying to scare Piggy, so I would have a bit of fun with this by deepening my pitch and slowing the pace, contrasting with what comes next].*

"It's come!" gasped Piggy. "It's real!" *[The word 'gasped' indicates that this will be high-pitched, fast and breathless].*

He clung to Ralph and reached to get his breath. *[I will drop the pace slightly to sustain the feeling of terror Piggy is feeling, but my pitch will be closer to moderate.]*

"Piggy, come outside. I want you Piggy." *[I will repeat the pitch and pace of the group of children to maintain the same identity as before and repeat this further down].*

Ralph's mouth was against Piggy's ear. *[I'm going to use moderate pitch and pace here and maintain it for Ralph's voice, with a slight drop in pitch to allow for gender difference between narrator and Ralph]*.

"Don't say anything."

"Piggy – where are you, Piggy?"

Something brushed against the back of the shelter. *[Moderate in both this and the next sentence]*.

Piggy kept still for a moment, then he had his asthma. He arched his back and crashed among the leaves with his legs. *[Moderate in both but the rate picks up, as there are more words to speak]*. Ralph rolled away from him. *[I will maintain a moderate pitch, but the pace will slow, both because there are few words but also because it brings the listener to a gentler close for the end of the passage]*.

It is always good to slow down as we speak the last phrase of any spoken presentation, and then pause before moving away or asking for questions. As an audience, we appreciate it as it brings us slowing 'into land' in our listening experience. If you listen to any piece of Classical or Baroque music, it will end with a three-chord sequence that brings us slowly to a stop as a listener.

Modulation pause

Pause is one of the most magical elements of modulation because it's the easiest, but one often overlooked. Yet it's so powerful. "During the pause, the meaning goes on" is a quote shared with me by my first drama teacher in South Africa[5] when I first learned about pause, and it's so true. The best composers master it and the same is true for speakers.

What is it? Pause is simply a short silence between words, phrases and sentences which add or enhance meaning to what is being said. I will introduce you to four pauses here, but you will most commonly use three for public speaking and other business purposes.

Sense pause – Long before writing was invented, we spoke groups of words, phrases or sentences, that made sense together, that made sense to the listener, that they could understand. As writing developed, so too were punctuation marks to help a reader understand how the words needed to be read together to be best understood. That importance for punctuation is becoming overlooked in the age of social media, where one often has to read and re-read a message to work out the phrasing, so the message makes sense. But hopefully, if you've experienced this, you understand the importance of punctuation. Here's an old chestnut to illustrate:

> *Woman without her man is nothing*
> *Woman, without her man, is nothing.*
> *Woman: without her, man is nothing.*

With the exact same words on the page, but with pauses in different places the sense of the words change. For practise in reading aloud, I recommend the following guidelines:

If it contains a comma, generally (, ; and :), this is about phrasing. Pause for one second.

If it contains a full stop (.?!), it's the end of thought or sentence. Pause for two seconds.

If you change to a different idea or thought, indicated in writing, by a paragraph, pause for three seconds.

You can use a forward slash (/) for each second paused and mark the text initially to help train yourself to pause.

Dramatic pause – This is a pause for effect and may be an addition to punctuation that is already there, or there may be no punctuation at all. A rhetorical question demands a slightly longer pause as we allow our audience to contemplate a response, but not too long as we don't want anyone to think it's an invitation to respond! An exclamation benefits from a somewhat longer pause as we want our audience to experience the surprise, delight or shock that we're expressing. Pause is an important tool to add emphasis to a word in a sentence. Here are a few examples for you to practise reading aloud:

Rhetorical question: What does this mean for the future? / /

Will you be a party to this? / /

Exclamation pause: No! We've got to draw a line in the sand.

Congratulations! / / No one deserved this more.

Emphasis: What will *we* / do to solve this problem?

What will we *do* / to solve this problem?

There are several ways to add emphasis and pause is just one. I'll take you through all of them under Modulation Emphasis, the final component of modulation below.

Circumstantial pause – this is a pause dictated by the audience and venue. I've already mentioned that we need to speak at the pace our audience will appreciate. I don't know what your primary school reading experience was. In the girls' convent school I attended, children rated themselves as good readers based on the speed of their delivery, perhaps because when we were learning we could only read slowly. As a result, fast reading was seen as good reading. This may inadvertently trickle into believing that fast speaking is smart speaking. Good speaking and smart speaking are actually speaking at the pace that allows your audience to enjoy listening! They can hear and process the information in a fairly relaxed manner. Pause adds to this experience.

It's also a good idea to pause before you begin. There are a couple of reasons for this. Often the audience are busy taking in your appearance and may miss your first few words – a common reason for forgetting people's names, I'm sure. Waiting on the audience gives them time to give you their full attention. It also gives you an opportunity to take a wonderful and full deep breath as you look out onto your audience and breathe the space. It's a good opportunity for a smile while you do this too! Two to three seconds should be sufficient.

Knowing how long to pause for laughter can be a challenge, especially as our practise potential for it is limited in our solo speech practises. In the comedy world what's known as comedic timing is a huge part of delivery and comedians will practise their jokes with various audiences to test the reaction and get a feel for timing of delivery. If you're tuned into your audience, you will listen for a lull – not complete silence, as you will lose audience energy and perhaps attention, but for the room to get just quiet enough for your words to be heard clearly again. Relaxation from the Rondo Sequence and some presence exercises, will ensure that you're relaxed and in tune with your audience, grasping this moment organically. While I pause, I tend to look at my audience and draw energy from the reaction. Never prepare or pause with the expectation of laughter, you may be disappointed. People tend to laugh in the most unexpected places when I speak and are sometimes silent where I expect laughter.

It's also necessary to take the venue acoustics into consideration. Outdoor venues require good use of pause as electronic speakers or the open air take time to transport the sound. Venues with an echo require the speaker to deliver in soundbites interspersed by pauses, so that the audience aren't hearing words on top of the echo from the previous phrase. I would highly recommend practising in a venue in advance to establish if there are any challenges such as these. It can be challenging to adjust our voices in the moment. It's also important for someone used to speaking in a challenging venue to adjust their voice for venues with good acoustics. It has been my experience that some religious leaders have learnt to speak in an echoing space and sound quite strange when speaking in a normal one, for instance.

Caesura pause – This is a balancing pause and is used in poetry. You may recite lines from a poem as part of a speech, so it is useful to know how to do them justice. Bob Geldof used lines by W.B. Yeats to great effect at an ISF keynote in 2020. Here's another short, beautiful poem by W.B. Yeats, selected by a groom I knew, in his speech several years ago:

> *'Had I the heavens' embroidered cloths,*
> *Enwrought with golden and silver light,*
> *The blue and the dim and the dark cloths*
> *Of night and light and the half-light,*

I would spread the cloths under your feet:
But I, being poor, have only my dreams;
I have spread my dreams under your feet;
Tread softly because you tread on my dreams.'

I've suggested how to pause for the punctuation you see in the poem. Each pause takes place after the preceding line. However, between lines three and four, there is none, so it would seem the right choice is to speak it as one phrase. It is called enjambment, from the French meaning to run on. But in order to express the shape of the verse as we speak it, we pause *on* the word 'cloths' before immediately running on to the next line. There is often then a caesura, or balancing pause, in the middle of that next line, and in this poem, it would naturally fall after the word 'light'. Play with reading it aloud and see how it sounds in a recording playback.

Exercise for pause

Returning to the *Lord of the Flies* passage, as it's familiar by now, aim to use as many varieties of pause as possible. Record yourself reading with pause and play it back to gauge the impact. I've included a marked-up copy of the first part here.

/ / / An extract from *Lord of the Flies* by William Golding / / /

"Listen. Listen for a long time." / / /

Quite clearly and emphatically, / and only a yard or so away from the back of the shelter, / a stick cracked. / / The blood roared again in Ralph's ears, / confused images chased each other through his mind. / / A composite of these things was prowling round the shelters. / / He could feel Piggy's head against his shoulder and the convulsive grip of a hand. / / /

"Ralph! Ralph!" / / /

"Shut up and listen." / / /

Desperately, / Ralph prayed that the beast would prefer littluns. / / /

Now, using the original passage, mark up the pauses you consider appropriate and practise reading it aloud.

Exercise for both pause and breath control

Here is a more difficult exercise for pause, which will challenge your breath control. The first sentence alone, in the sample text, is 82 words long, requiring the judicious use of both.

An extract from 'The Pickwick Papers' by Charles Dickens.[6]

'A casual observer, adds the secretary, to whose notes we are indebted for the following account – a casual observer might possibly have remarked nothing extraordinary in the bald head, and circular spectacles, which were intently turned towards his (the secretary's) face, during the reading of the above resolutions: to those who knew that the gigantic brain of Pickwick was working beneath that forehead, and that the beaming eyes of Pickwick were twinkling behind those glasses, the sight was indeed an interesting one. There sat the man who had traced to their source the mighty ponds of Hampstead and agitated the scientific world with his Theory of Tittlebats, as calm and unmoved as the deep waters of the one on a frosty day, or as a solitary specimen of the other in the inmost recesses of an earthen jar. And how much more interesting did the spectacle become, when, starting into full life and animation, as a simultaneous call for "Pickwick" burst from his followers, that illustrious man slowly mounted into the Windsor chair, on which he had been previously seated, and addressed the club he himself had founded. What a study for an artist did that exciting scene present! The eloquent Pickwick, with one hand gracefully concealed behind his coat tails, and the other waving in air, to assist his glowing declamation; his elevated position revealing those tights and gaiters, which, had they clothed an ordinary man, might have passed without observation, but which, when Pickwick clothed them – if we may use the expression – inspired voluntary awe and respect; surrounded by the men who had volunteered to share the perils of his travels, and who were destined to participate in the glories of his discoveries.'

Modulation tone

Tone is the general quality of the voice and is produced in the resonators. It comprises *tone amount,* which is the volume of our speech and *tone colour,* which is its quality.

Tone volume is how loudly or softly we speak. It is often confused with projection. Most of us have experienced teachers who told pupils to speak louder in order to be heard. I know that the same instruction is given in schools today. Like pace, most of us grow up learning what is considered moderate volume by their family standards. There are some very loud-speaking families and some where everyone speaks quietly to each other.

As you speak and read aloud, it's a good exercise to think about when, what, and why your vocal volume increases and decreases to express more meaning to your listener or produce different responses from them. Contrast in volume can be a powerful tool to engage your listener. In a classroom management book[7] I was recommended during an English-teaching stint at a school, the author spoke about the power of speaking quietly to a room of students to get their attention. Why? Because of the need to quieten down to hear. It also has a calming effect, opposite to the effect of shouting.

If you speak louder, you create an emotional response in your audience. A terrible illustration of this is heard in recordings of Adolf Hitler's speeches in Nazi Germany. I have no idea what he is saying, thankfully, but he carried the crowds on a wave of hope and excitement that clearly inspired them. The experience with which I grew up was fortunately quite innocuous, unless you were a gambler. The voice that engendered excitement in many when I was a child was that of a racing commentator in a horse race.[8] The commentator spoke at a pace that was barely comprehensible and his volume, pitch and pace rose as the race drew to a close. It can literally increase your heartbeat.

This is effective for a sport's setting as the race reaches a crescendo. It's highly effective and engaging but should be used with care in public speaking. Patsy Rodenburg once said that a person can listen to a shouty voice for 90 seconds before switching off. Sadly, I have heard some evangelical preachers in Africa and the US who speak too loudly when they preach. It's unfortunate and I would caution against it for reasons already explained.

There is another important reason. A person using increased volume to be heard lacks vocal variety. Not only are they not varying their volume but it's unlikely they are varying the other elements of modulation as their vocal strength is directed in this one area.

Exercise for tone volume

Revisit the *Lord of the Flies* extract and look for opportunities for increasing and decreasing volume. When marking a text, I tend to use an up or down arrow to denote where I need to increase and decrease volume. You can also use the following musical terms, which are the Latin for loud and quiet.

s – quietly

ss – very quietly

f – loudly

ff – very

loudlym - moderate

If you would prefer to work with a new piece of writing, here's another extract from *The Pickwick Papers* that lends itself admirably to volume changes. I will provide a second copy of the paragraph, leaving the first for you to work on.

An extract from The Pickwick Papers by Charles Dickens

> 'The sport was at its height, the sliding was at the quickest, the laughter was at the loudest, when a sharp smart crack was heard. There was a quick rush towards the bank, a wild scream from the ladies, and a shout from Mr. Tupman. A large mass of ice disappeared; the water bubbled up over it; Mr. Pickwick's hat, gloves, and handkerchief were floating

> *on the surface; and this was all of Mr. Pickwick that*
> *anybody could see.*
>> *Dismay and anguish were depicted on every countenance, the*
>> *males turned pale, and the females fainted, Mr Snodgrass*
>> *and Mr. Winkle grasped each other by the hand, and gazed*
>> *at the spot where their leader had gone down, with frenzied*
>> *eagerness: while Mr. Tupman, by way of rendering the*
>> *promptest assistance, and at the same time conveying to*
>> *any persons who might be within hearing the clearest*
>> *possible notion of the catastrophe, ran off across the country*
>> *at his utmost speed, screaming "Fire!" with all his might.'*

This is an idea of tone and volume variations I might make. Please note that these would be heard as subtle variations across the piece and with the additional benefit of the other aspects of modulation, pace in particular:

> (m) *The sport was at its height,* (mf) *the sliding was at the*
> *quickest,* (f) *the laughter was at the loudest,* (m) *when a*
> *sharp smart crack was heard.* (mf) *There was a quick rush*
> *towards the bank,* (ff) *a wild scream from the ladies,* (mf)
> *and a shout from Mr. Tupman.* (m) *A large mass of ice*
> *disappeared;* (ms) *the water bubbled up over it; Mr.*
> *Pickwick's hat, gloves, and handkerchief were floating on*
> *the surface;* (s) *and this was all of Mr. Pickwick that*
> *anybody could see.*

Tone colour is the quality, mood or emotion conveyed in the words. I don't imagine many of us have passed through our childhood or teen years without hearing at least once, "Don't speak to me in that tone of voice?" Or were you ever told by a parent or teacher to change your tone? I can also distinctly remember my siblings being admonished for being mean, and their response, "I only said ..." devoid of the tone that had so upset me. This should demonstrate the power that tone has on how we speak.

Because we speak from a combination of our thoughts and feelings, this naturally colours our voice as we express ourselves. We naturally use our tone to express, for example, delight or dissatisfaction. To quote Newton's Third Law in Power: "Every action has an equal and opposite reaction." In public speaking, we speak to elicit a reaction or response. Otherwise, why say it? Even a rather bland public announcement such as "This is the News at Ten" is designed to elicit a response and the tone is deliberately neutral. One of the issues with a practised speech or response is that it can lack emotional engagement because the speaker has forgotten the emotions behind their words.

The connection exercises covered in section 2 will ensure the voice is emotionally connected but it's important to recall the emotion in what you're saying and express it again so that you connect with your listening audience. I can recall interviews where candidates are asked increasingly challenging questions because it's clear their practised responses are not landing with the panel. When it comes to speeches and presentations, an audience can experience a response of 'I don't believe you' or 'You don't care' if you're not engaging emotionally with the words and conveying that in your tone.

Also, remember the soft palate exercises from the same section: even if it's not appropriate to smile, lifting the soft palate creates a warmer, more connected voice. Tone colour will change throughout our presentation as will the tone of the different responses in an interview. You will also use the other aspects of modulation to express these too.

Questions to help with tone colour

- What adjectives would I use to describe what I've prepared to say?

Here are a few suggestions to start with but do add your own to match your message:

informative, persuasive, humorous, serious, enthusiastic,
delighted, angry, knowledgeable

- How do I want my audience to respond? What do I want my audience to think, feel and/or do as a result of my words?
- What can I do to ensure I'm eliciting the response I want from my audience?

The answer to the third question can be to change the words, or sometimes, it's just to change your tone.

- Are there opportunities for changes in tone colour?

Exercise for tone colour

Here are two extracts to help you think about tone colour. It's extraordinary to realise that these were penned about 170 years ago and yet we can infuse them with meaning today, just by speaking them aloud with expression. Think about how you feel as you read the words. What do you think Dickens was thinking and feeling, and how might he want his audience to respond? Read it aloud to convey what you believe to be the right tone, using what you know about pitch, pace and pause already.

An extract from *Bleak House* by Charles Dickens

> 'Fog everywhere. Fog up the river, where it flows among green
> aits and meadows; fog down the river, where it rolls defiled
> among the tiers of shipping, and the waterside pollutions of
> a great (and dirty) city. Fog on the Essex Marshes, fog on
> the Kentish heights. Fog creeping into the cabooses of
> collier-brigs; fog lying out on the yards and hovering in the
> rigging of great ships; fog drooping on the gunwales of
> barges and small boats. Fog in the eyes and throats of
> ancient Greenwich pensioners, wheezing by the firesides of
> their wards; fog in the stem and bowl of the afternoon pipe
> of the wrathful skipper, down in his close cabin; fog cruelly
> pinching the toes and fingers of his shivering little 'prentice
> boy on deck. Chance people on the bridges peeping over the
> parapets into a nether sky of fog, with fog all round them,

as if they were up in a balloon and hanging in the misty clouds.'

An extract from *Bleak House* by Charles Dickens

> *'Sir Leicester Dedlock is only a baronet, but there is no mightier baronet than he. His family is as old as the hills, and infinitely more respectable. He has a general opinion that the world might get on without hills but would be done up without Dedlocks. He would on the whole admit Nature to be a good idea (a little low, perhaps, when not enclosed with a park-fence), but an idea dependent for its execution on your great county families. He is a gentleman of strict conscience, disdainful of all littleness and meanness, and ready, on the shortest notice, to die any death you may please to mention rather than give occasion for the least impeachment of his integrity. He is an honourable, obstinate, truthful, high-spirited, intensely prejudiced, perfectly unreasonable man.*
> *Sir Leicester is twenty years, full measure, older than my Lady. He will never see sixty-five again, nor perhaps sixty-six, nor yet sixty-seven. He has a twist of the gout now and then and walks a little stiffly. He is of a worthy presence, with his light grey hair and whiskers, his fine shirt-frill, his pure white waistcoat, and his blue coat with bright buttons always buttoned. He is ceremonious, stately, most polite on every occasion to my Lady, and holds her personal attractions in the highest estimation. His gallantry to my Lady, which has never changed since he courted her, is the one little touch of romantic fancy in him.'*

I believe Dickens wanted to convey the pervasive sense of oppression created by fog in the first passage and he uses repetition of the word 'fog' and longer vowel sounds to convey this. It's easier to feel it when you read aloud. The second passage seem to be much brighter in tone and the shorter vowel sounds help convey this. I also believe it's satirical. The content of both passages help communicate the mood as well as the words and the punctuation.

Now think about your message. It might be helpful to record your ideas when you're preparing a presentation. Give yourself permission to record them with the emotional conviction as if before your audience. The great leaders would have dictated their messages aloud and it would have fallen to a secretary to commit them to a page in black and white. I contend that one of the challenges we have today is that we're in danger of murdering our speeches before they have life if we capture them first in black and white on screen or page.

One good reason for using humour in a speech is that it automatically provides a change in tone colour. There are many opportunities for light and shade in a presentation. Look for them and include them. It's one more technique for keeping your audience engaged.

Modulation inflection

The penultimate element of modulation zooms in to look at how we can change our voice within a word. Inflection influences how our words can be interpreted or misinterpreted and should therefore not be underestimated or overlooked.

Inflection can be defined as the gentle rise and fall of the voice on syllables. We are bending the shape of words to instil meaning. There are several ways we can do this. While the inflection could be on one word in an entire sentence, I will illustrate with one word alone for simplicity and include the symbols I would use over the syllable or word if I were marking a text for reading aloud.

- *Rising inflection (/)*: we can inflect up on the second syllable, e.g., "Par<u>don</u>?"
- *Falling inflection (\\)*: inflecting down, where the second syllable is lower than the first, e.g., "Noth<u>ing</u>."
- *Compound rising inflection (v):* where the middle syllable(s) can be lower than the first and last syllable, e.g., "Ab<u>solute</u>ly!"
- *Compound falling inflection(^)*: the first and last syllable can be lower than the middle syllable(s), e.g., "Dis<u>appoint</u>ing."

- *Circumflex inflection (~)*: this is where the voice snakes within the word, e.g., "Str~a~nge?!"

This might seem like too much information, and you may never use these for the majority of your public speaking requirements. But firstly, it's possible you're using all of them already. Secondly, if you are aware of them, you're more likely to access them for increasing your engagement with your audience.

Exercise for inflection: Oh!

I believe this exercise beautifully illustrates the power of inflection. Even if you were to record it with just sound, a word can carry so much meaning if we express the thought behind it fully.

Play with each of these as you express the thought aloud, using only the word 'Oh'. Even better, ask someone to work with you and guess what you're thinking as you express your 'Oh'.

Now, ask them to do the same and see if you can guess what they're thinking or feeling. Remember, words are spoken in a context, so you might wish to create the context first. I've made suggestions in brackets to create the thought that might motivate the expression.

This list of suggestions, while comprehensive, is not exhaustive.

1. Acknowledgement "Oh (I hear you)!"
2. Affectionate "Oh (I'm so happy for you)!"
3. Anger "Oh (I'm going to kill someone)!"
4. Anguish "Oh (I'll never get that promotion)!"
5. Annoyance "Oh (Stupid car/computer/desk)!"
6. Blissful "Oh (A mouthful of my favourite food)!"
7. Compassion "Oh (Poor you)!"
8. Delight "Oh (You got me tickets)!"
9. Despair "Oh (It's never going to happen)!"
10. Disbelief "Oh (You never)!"
11. Doubt/Confusion "Oh (I'm not sure about that)!"
12. Disapproval "Oh (You shouldn't have done that)"
13. Ecstatic "Oh (*Another* promotion)!"

14. Embarrassment "Oh (I was picking my nose)!"
15. Flirtatious "Oh (I know you like me)"
16. Frustration "Oh (The network is down)!"
17. Horror "Oh (You pranged my car)!"
18. Fear "Oh (You gave me a fright)!"
19. Idea "Oh (I've thought of a solution)!"
20. Pain "Oh (Instead of 'ouch')!"
21. Realisation "Oh (I understand now)!"
22. Shock "Oh (I wasn't expecting that)!"
23. Surprise "Oh (What a wonderful surprise)!"
24. Suspicion "Oh (Is that so)?"
25. Sympathy "Oh (I'm so sorry for you)!"
26. Relief "Oh (Here at last)!"
27. Trouble "Oh-oh (I'm/you're in trouble now)!"
28. Wistfulness "Oh (I wish I could have that)!"

Inflection can be used to add humour to your talk. Satire, sarcasm and deadpan are often expressed entirely through inflection or lack thereof. *John and Marsha* by Stan Freberg was a single released by Capitol Records in the United States in 1951 with only two words – 'John' and 'Marsha'. It's a wonderful illustration of the power of inflection. Apparently, it was banned by the BBC because at some point in the 2:30-minute single it implied an inappropriate relationship between the characters, even though both voices were that of Freberg and only two words, both proper nouns, were spoken. That is a testimony to the power of voice!

Modulation emphasis

When we step up to speak, we hopefully do it because we have something important to say that is worth sharing. But within that message, there are some words and phrases we consider more important than others. We use emphasis to show this. Emphasis is also necessary at times for meaning and changing emphasis can change the meaning of what we're saying entirely. I have been told that an Imam chants the Quran without inflection or emphasis to avoid adding meaning to the holy words.

Chapter 11

Emphasis is the way of making a word or phrase stand out to bring out a certain meaning in a sentence. It can be achieved through an increase in tone volume, through inflection, with a pause, by use of repetition and non-verbally through gesture. To illustrate, and recall how you probably use emphasis every day, try the following exercise.

Exercise 1 for emphasis

"Where were you for today's meeting?"

Tone volume: Say one word of the above question louder than the rest of the sentence, i.e., "Where were *you* for today's meeting?" Repeat with a different word spoken louder. Do you see how the meaning has changed?

Inflection: use circumflex inflection to add curiosity to 'were' in the above question, i.e., "Where *were* you for today's meeting?"

Pause: Stop for a split second after 'today's' in the question, e.g., "Where were you for today's / meeting?"

Repetition: This is a common and powerful tool to add emphasis, so much so that 'The Rule of Three' or 'The Power of Three' are commonly recommended for speech writing where the speaker is encouraged to repeat their point in three different ways. An example with this sentence might be, "Where were you for today's meeting? Where? Tell me?"

Gesture: Think of what gesture you might naturally use if you were to say this to a member of your team or a colleague. Because of the added power of body language, I don't imagine myself using body language with a more senior figure than myself when asking this question. An example I can suggest for added emphasis would be to lift one's shoulders and turning palms upward on 'where' in the above question.

In truth, we can use some or all these simultaneously to emphasise what we're communicating. In a planned and practised speech, it might be worthwhile video-recording a conversation with someone and play it back to note what tools of emphasis you naturally use every day. If you're self-conscious about doing that, watch someone you admire being interviewed instead.

Inflection is closely linked to tone. We colour our tone within a word. Have you heard of a loaded statement? Even a word can be loaded. It starts in our mind with the thought or feeling we're having and if we don't filter it to consider the effect it might have on audiences, we need to take responsibility for what happens next.

Exercise 2 for emphasis: the power of words and voice together

I find this a fun exercise for emphasis, and it demonstrates how meaning changes as we change emphasis. If you feel like having a play, why not make up your own sentence chain and see how many links you can add? It's also interesting to alternate speaking these with someone else.

- I am.
- I am too.
- I am too qualified.
- I am far too qualified.
- I am far too qualified for that.
- I am far too qualified for that position.
- I am far too qualified for that position there.
- No, I am far too qualified for that position there.
- No, I am not far too qualified for that position there.
- No, I am not far too qualified for that position there now.
- No, Gillian, I am not far too qualified for that position there now.
- No, Gillian, I am not far too qualified for that particular position there now.
- *(Repeat, but with emphasis on different words)*

As an aside, you may have noted that you increased your speaking rate for longer sentences. It didn't take twice as long to speak twelve words as six. You can use this in your speech writing. A shorter sentence can have more impact and emphasis just because it stands out amidst longer ones.

When you have a presentation to work with, think carefully about where you want to add emphasis. It's a great tool of vocal variety that utilises several components, as you can see. A word of warning: don't overdo it! A speaker who tries to emphasise everything, ends up emphasising nothing, as the audience loses track of what's most important. I've only come across this once in more than two decades, and it's easy to correct with awareness, but it's better not to start doing it at all.

Now bring it all together

You now have six aspects of modulation at your disposal that will ensure you engage more effectively with your audience.

Chapter 12
How Can I Speak with Clarity?

By now, you have several techniques with which to engage and connect with your audience, in addition to speaking with power and confidence. But what about clarity? How clear is your speech? Do people understand you, or ask you to repeat yourself?

I believe we're made for community and people, especially professionals, and can be quite tolerant of poorly formed speech. When we listen, we expend energy tuning into people. Those of us who have travelled widely or hosted many travellers are accommodating of accents, languages and various idioms of speech that are unfamiliar. But what if when we speak, our audience didn't have to expend so much energy on listening and engaging? What if we, as speakers, learned to speak clearly and thoughtfully so that listeners could invest more energy in engaging with the message?

If you want to make listening an effortless task for your audience, clarity of speech is vital. I don't believe we invest enough in this. Television and film are presenting more and more actors who mumble, and we are obliged to use volume and subtitles to compensate. Thankfully, the standards are still being maintained on stage in theatres and, for the most part, at conferences.

Chapter 12

What does clear speech sound like, outside the remit of a Speech Therapist, who deals with congenital or accident-related issues? If we brainstorm the barriers to clear speech, it might be easier to think about this. Think of what gets in the way for you when others are listening to you and when you are listening to others. They might include the following:

- Speaking through a partially closed mouth. Laziness or poor habit could cause this. See jaw exercises in Chapter Six.
- A hand that partially or habitually covers the mouth. This can be a poor habit or self-consciousness. Self-awareness and a decision to do something else with our hands can help. A suggested default mode for hands is covered in Chapter Four, under Posture.
- Lack of practise. Genuinely, some people avoid speaking unless they must. Others, such as those living alone, can spend days without speaking to someone. Reading Aloud in Chapter 10 offers an antidote to this.
- Speaking too quickly and swallowing some words. See Pace in Chapter 11.
- Accent. This will be covered in Chapter 13.
- A habit of mumbling. This is poor or lazy articulation.

Articulation examined

Most of how we present ourselves to the world is based on habit, whether it's speaking to family, friends, or the wider world. Our human nature is to do as little as possible to accomplish what we need. So, if everyone understands what we're saying in our world, why change it? However, an opportunity to speak to an audience of mostly strangers requires us to raise our game. In speaking terms, this means elevating our speech. Fortunately, this is not difficult. The challenge is to do it so that it's authentic. The three exercises below will help. If you practise these, I guarantee you will see results. More to the point, your audience will experience the results.

Exercise 1: Over-articulation

Take your two minutes reading aloud exercise for the day. Over-articulate the first line, then speak the second. Over articulation is exaggerating the shape of every word and giving each word equal weight. We naturally don't place emphasis on less important words, such as 'and', 'the' or 'as', but this exercise means every word matters. If you like, imagine you're speaking to someone through soundproof glass who desperately needs to understand you. Here's an example to try with:

"The key to this door is in the top-left-hand drawer. I have to get out by eight for the dentist."

Over-articulating forces us to open our jaw wider and move our lips in a far more animated fashion. When we speak our next sentence normally, the pronunciation of each word will be just a little bit better. Repeat the over-articulated sentence above and follow with this, in your usual voice:

"I hope they find it so they can let me out."

Often, the letters that suffer most through poor articulation are d and t, but it can vary based on accent. I've deliberately included both letters above.

Here is an extract from Shakespeare to practise more. I've avoided including The Bard any sooner as many people have had a negative experience of Shakespeare in school. But he is a master of language, word sound and shape, as well as putting the right words together. If you can just read it as you would eat an exquisite meal; you don't have to know the ingredients to enjoy it! Just trust me and chew on his words. I recommend a minimum of four lines at a time, with two lines of over-articulation, followed by two lines spoken with your normal speaking voice. I've italicised the 'normal' sentence to make it easier.

> Portia: *The quality of mercy is not strained;*
> *It droppeth as the gentle rain from heaven*
> Upon the place beneath. It is twice blest;

It blesseth him that gives and him that takes:
'T is mightiest in the mightiest; it becomes
The throned monarch better than his crown:
His sceptre shows the force of temporal power,
The attribute to awe and majesty,
Wherein doth sit the dread and fear of kings;
But mercy is above this sceptred sway;
It is enthroned in the hearts of kings,
It is an attribute to God himself;
And earthly power doth then show likest God's
When mercy seasons justice.[1]

Exercise 2: Whispering into speaking

The next articulation exercise is to whisper into speaking. Whispering is different to speaking, in that the vocal cords are not engaged. It's speaking in a hushed tone just using the breath and organs of speech (See Fig 5). Take four to eight lines from the passage above or another of your choice and whisper the first two lines and speak the second two. Whispering requires us to exaggerate the shape of our words in order to be heard and understood.

Exercise 3: Chanting into speaking

Chanting is also a brilliant way of warming up your voice quickly if you don't have a lot of time. The most well-known context for chanting today is probably supporters chanting their team's name or songs and chanting at protest marches. I would suggest that a lot of that is closer to shouting though and advise against basing your chanting on these models! The origin of chanting is, in both Eastern and Western religion, associated with monks and nuns and often taking place in buildings where the acoustics enhance the sound. It is not usually accompanied by instruments.

To do this yourself, simply pitch your voice higher than usual and intone on one note. When you feel more confident, chant the notes above and below if you wish. Just play with it. Feel free to elongate the vowels. No one needs a good singing voice to do this, so don't let that get in the way. You can do this in your home language, but the beauty of doing it in Latin or another language which you don't understand is that you're less likely to feel the need to place emphasis on particular words or syllables.[2]

> *A Do-mi-no fact-um est Be-ne-dic-tus*
> *Con-cer-tuum lat-in-o-sac-ro-rum: A Do-m-in-o fact-um est*
> *De-us me-us es tu et con-fi-te-bor ti-bi*
> *O mag-num mys-te-ri-um*
> *Et ad-mi-ra-bi-le sac-ra-men-tum*
> *Ut an-im-al-i-a vi-de-rent Do-m-in-um na-tum*
> *Ja-cen-tem in pra-es-ep-i-o*
> *Be-a-ta Vir-go cu-jus vis-ce-ra*
> *Me-ru-er-unt por-ta-re*
> *Do-m-in-um Chris-tum Al-le-lu-ia*

Resonance Scale revisited

The Resonance Scale, is also an exercise in speech clarity, especially for vowel sounds and monophthongs – vowel sounds that are made with one mouth shape to create one vowel sound. The sentence that ends that exercise

> *Who would know aught of art must first learn and then take his ease.*

is also useful for articulation. So, you can have three for the price of one with that exercise, as it helps with resonance, pitch and articulation!

Chapter 13
What Can I Do About My Accent?

What is accent and what impact does it have?

Accent is a highly emotive subject. At the date of writing, accent is not a protected category in discrimination legislation in the UK. Yet there are stories of people who face discrimination because of their accent in colleges, universities, and the workplace every week. The traditional portrayal of accent in film contributes to certain stereotypes and this can filter into our behaviour towards people who speak differently to us.

For the purposes of illustration, here are a few examples of accent stereotypes I have grown up with in films I've watched over the years. Costume, age and gender also play a part, but I've tried to keep it simple. I've listed the accent first, the negative stereotype second:

- Irish – naive, not very bright
- London – sleazy, underhand (male)
- Southern States, USA – backward
- Russian male – untrustworthy, gangster
- Oxbridge – educated, classy
- French – smooth, romantic
- Italian – passionate, volatile

- German – cold, calculating

I'm confident you could add to this list. When it comes to employability and promotion, you can see how these stereotypes of people's accents don't serve employers or employees. Much of this discrimination is subliminal. And within each country, having a northern, southern, rural or city dialect can add layers to the perception, dialect being a form of language that's particular to a region or social group.

It will therefore not surprise you to hear that a percentage of my clients come to me because they have a problem with their accent. Or more to the point, they experience other people having a problem with their accent. It can create a barrier when your accent is in the minority.

So, what is accent? Accent can be defined simply and accurately as a distinctive way of pronouncing a language, often associated with a particular country, area or community. However, I think of it as so much more. **Accent is the personality of the voice, the womb language, the rhythm and cadence of the birth culture.** It becomes everything we absorb as we grow, move and interact with others. It can include its volume and pace. It's what introduced you to the sound of the human world before you were born, even if the world into which you entered and grew spoke a different language.

How could that be bad or wrong?

It will therefore come as no surprise that I am a huge fan of accent diversity. But we all acknowledge that diversity comes with a call to make a greater effort to understand and to be understood. Accent demands this too.

If we consider language the distinctive means by which humans communicate, local accent can be a barrier to communicating to a wider audience. It is therefore vital that as listeners, we learn to tune our ears to a variety of accents and as speakers, that we learn to speak in a way that is accessible to a wider audience. Because this book is for English speakers and those wishing to speak English, this is where my focus lies. I'm also conscious that this is so much easier to hear and speak about than to read and write about. I will therefore limit the scope of this to some basic ideas I hope you will find helpful.

RP English (Received Pronunciation) is an accent

What has been considered the best English has changed over the last century. In the Commonwealth at least, the Queen's English was considered something to aspire to up to the post war years. As television became popular and widespread, a slightly more natural tone became popular, known as BBC English. It's only really since the 1980s that recognition was given to a wider variety of accents and gradually Received Pronunciation, known as RP English, became more popular and acceptable.

I would like to offer a definition of RP English as **speaking in such a way that your audience can understand you**. However, who are you to know what your audience understands? You would need to speak in a neutral accent to be understood by everyone who understands English. If you used phonetics to pronounce every English word you speak, you would be speaking RP English. It is therefore an accent, not a dialect since all RP speakers speak Standard English.

Because I believe in coaching people to show up as their authentic selves and believe strongly in diversity, I take issue with encouraging people to sound homogeneous. Listening to some BBC radio archive footage, you can hear how wrong this sounds. One particularly funny clip I discovered is a discussion on sex education from the '80s between a schoolteacher, the interviewer and a couple of teenagers. They all sound the same and are talking about sex so politely and neutrally – it's funny, but sad. They seem devoid of character and personality and it's a challenge to tell them apart from each other, except for gender.

Therefore, it is my suggestion that you learn the basics of Standard/RP English pronunciation and allow it to influence your spoken words while still honouring your accent as an authentic element of who you are. The articulation exercises in the previous chapter will ensure that you speak with crispness and clarity. It's helpful to take every opportunity to speak with people who have crisp, clear voices as this will be a comfortable environment into which you can speak better. I acknowledge that it's an essential skill for actors to speak RP as standard, excuse the pun, but that it's not required for everyone. It is useful, however, to access a good, clear standard of English for public speaking.

A story or three

During a workshop, Patsy Rodenburg told us a story of a young black actor in her class who was dismissive of the benefits of RP English. He spoke in what is now referred to as Multicultural London English (MLE), similar to Stormzy, the British rapper. As he was driving a nice car, police officers would regularly pull him over to check his credentials. One evening, tired of this, he switched to speaking RP as soon as he lowered his window. The officers immediately apologised and sent him on his way.

I heard that story in the late 1990s. Now I realise that it speaks much more to the prejudices of people than the benefits of speaking RP. But only this year, I heard a similar story of an African colleague who switches on her RP when white people queue-jump in front of her. Their response to her voice? Instant apologies. It's appalling that anyone should need to do that to express equity and it should be unnecessary to feed people's prejudices. But sometimes, you do what you must do to get by.

On the flip side, I've experienced reverse prejudice due to my accent. In Ireland, publicans have a respected status because they are property owners and businesspeople, involved in the commerce of the local community. Often their children attend boarding school because of the business hours, and generally live over the large premises. My dad, who was a publican, wore tailored suits every day of his life. You get the picture, I hope. In the UK, however, most pubs are owned by breweries and run by landlords and landladies. In a highly class-ridden society, this is considered less worthy of equal regard. Since living in the UK, I've experienced many a surprised look or barely supressed raised eyebrow when I declare in my combination RP/Irish/South African accent that I'm an Irish publican's daughter.

Because it's so subtle, I've never felt able to question anyone, but I imagine they are surprised such a seemingly respectable person comes from a somewhat disreputable background!

By now, you will hopefully realise that the work which needs to be done is as much on the part of the listener as the speaker.

Below, you will see a selection of tongue twisters. They are often used and recommended indiscriminately, particularly by online vocal coaches I've heard. I generally reserve them for younger students or clients wishing to moderate their accent and increase speech clarity. While they provide a fun way to practise articulation, I prefer the exercises in Chapter 12 for my adult first-language-English speakers. I will generally select specific tongue twisters based on the letters that a client is struggling with but if you go through these you should watch out for the follow letters and ensure you're not mixing them up:

- V and w as in *vent* and *went*.
- W and wh as in *were* and *where*.
- T for *tent* and th for *then*. Or a combination for start and endings of words such as *tenth* and *that*.
- F instead of th in *think* and *thank*.

Tongue twister exercise

These are good for your brain as well as your speech and they might even make you or others laugh! As you go through them, think about the letters, words and word endings you find most challenging and focus on those when you revisit them. I've given some indication in italics of the focus of each tongue twister, without using complicated terms[1]. Sometimes it's the transition from a word ending in one consonant to beginning with another. Seek to read them with clarity, fluency and confidence. Read them slowly until you can speak them at a moderate pace.

By now, I hope you realise that reading them aloud is not optional!

Chapter 13

(b, endings)	A box of biscuits, a batch of mixed biscuits.
(s, st, sk, endings)	A skunk sat on a stump and thunk the stump stunk, but the stump thunk the skunk stunk.
(vowels)	Unique New York.
(vowels, endings)	Red lorry, yellow lorry, red lorry, yellow lorry.
(s, th, st, x, transitions)	Six thick thistle sticks. Six thick thistles stick.
(b, vowels)	A big black bug bit a big black bear, made the big black bear bleed blood.
(two vowel sounds)	*Toy* boat. Toy boat. Toy boat. Old oily Ollie oils old oily autos.
(sl, sh)	*I* slit the sheet, the sheet I slit, and on the slitted sheet I sit.
(sh, s, vowels)	Shy Shelly says she shall sew sheets.
(t)	A Tudor who tooted a flute tried to tutor two tooters to toot. Said the two to their tutor, "Is it harder to toot or to tutor two tooters to toot?"
(th, fr, thr)	Three free throws.
(s, sh, transitions)	Mrs. Smith's Fish Sauce Shop.
(transitions)	*Which* wristwatches are Swiss wristwatches?
(er, th, tt, transitions)	Lesser leather never weathered wetter weather better.
(consonants)	Knapsack straps.
(oi, oy)	A noisy noise annoys an oyster.
(th,,t)	The myth of Miss Muffet.
(v)	Vincent vowed vengeance very vehemently.
(w)	How much wood would a woodchuck chuck if a woodchuck could chuck wood? He would chuck, he would, as much as he could, and chuck as much wood as a woodchuck would if a woodchuck could chuck wood.

(ch, sh, tr)	Cheap ship trip.
(s, vowels)	Mr. See owned a saw. And Mr. Soar owned a seesaw. Now See's saw sawed Soar's seesaw Before Soar saw See, Which made Soar sore.
(f, fl, fr)	Friendly Frank flips fine flapjacks.
	Fat frogs flying past fast.
	Flee from fog to fight flu fast!
(l, transitions)	Lovely lemon liniment.
(t, th, tw)	Tim, the thin twin tinsmith.
(gr, transition)	Greek grapes.
(b, bl)	The boot black bought the black boot back.
	Black bug's blood.
(m, n, sh, ch)	*Moose noshing much mush.*
(tw)	Twelve twins twirled twelve twigs.
(endings)	Don't pamper damp scamp tramps
	that camp under ramp lamps.
(st, ch, sh)	If Stu chews shoes, should Stu
	choose the shoes he chews?
(cr, endings)	Crisp crusts crackle crunchily.

Now that you know where your strengths and challenges lie with different words, consider changing some phrases in your speech or presentation so that you can present your best self. For example, I avoid the words 'reciprocity' because I fail to say it with panache, but I have no problem with saying 'reciprocal behaviour' or 'reciprocal relationship'.

Chapter 13

Just for fun, let's end with a few traditional tongue twisters that challenge smooth transitions and articulation.

A proper cup of coffee in a proper copper coffee cup.

You've no need to light a night-light
On a light night like tonight,
For a night-light's light's a slight light,
And tonight's a night that's light.
When a night's light, like tonight's light,
It is really not quite right
To light night-lights with their slight lights
On a light night like tonight.

SECTION FOUR

What more can I do?

Chapter 14
Introduction - The 'Hair And Make-up' Of Presenting

By now, you've gathered all the tools in your toolbox for 'below the waterline' work on your voice, your speech and the body language and presence required to engage your audience, no matter what the situation requires. Now it is time to look at what's 'above the waterline', what I like to call the hair and make-up of presenting yourself to an audience. The following chapters in this section include:

- Planning your content
- Audience Considerations
- Timings
- Resources and tools
- The Curveballs

In this section, the scope of public speaking includes facilitating as well as presenting at in person and online meetings, as well as speeches or talks. In my experience, subject matter experts and leaders are often in a position where they are called on to facilitate others in their opportunities for 'public speaking', albeit amongst peers or within their organisations exclusively. I have taken the liberty to cover the aspects of meeting facilitation; I have seen them provide unnecessary obstacles to positive speaking opportunities.

Chapter 14

As I've headed the chapter with the term 'hair and make-up', what about the actual hair and make-up of presenting? And what about clothing?

My favourite rule of thumb is drawn from Nancy Kline's writing about Place as a component of a Thinking Environment©. Place is about our environment but it's also about our appearance. It needs to say to the other person, or the audience, 'you matter'. If we think about this, if we ask ourselves, *Will they know they matter because of how I have prepared my outward appearance for this meeting?* I believe we are unlikely to get it wrong. You will find further writing and my experience of Place in Section Five.

Traditionally, hair and make-up has been a low stress question for those identifying as male, as the professional look from the '50s onwards was a suit and tie, hair short back and sides. Fortunately, the 21st century, with more equality across gender, age, culture, and class has brought more liberty to the traditionally male look. And more women in leadership globally have also provided a broader range of role models, although I've found the media to be both old-fashioned and harsh when judging anyone who's not a white heterosexual Western male.

It would be tempting to encourage you to play it safe, not to take chances. However, I encourage you to be authentic to yourself, your identity, and your message with a consideration for what your audience will find helpful. If you believe, as we established in Chapter One that the priority for effective communication is audience first, then message and then you, the speaker, you cannot ignore the opportunity your appearance may present to support, or hinder, your message. It's about the role you are presenting and what your appearance needs to say for that role.

Let me provoke your thinking with a few examples. When I took my practical Speech and Drama exams, we were encouraged to wear simple black clothing. I encouraged my students to do the same. Why? It's about focus. We were being assessed, judged, marked, on our performance – physical and vocal. Our ability to embody the character, be it a character from Greek mythology or an American college student, needed to impress the examiner through our movement and voice. Anything other than a plain colour carried the likelihood of distraction or interpretation. We need to embody our message for an audience when we speak. What role are you speaking from and how do you support that in how you dress? Scientific expert? Thought leader? HR Director?

I hope the simplicity suggested above provides a baseline for you to consider how to dress. All black is something of a blank canvas for performers. All black may have different associations for your audience, especially culturally, but if it is authentic to you, that may be acceptable. I would always caution you to ensure this is not a great choice if your stage or screen backdrop is black! A suit for a person identifying as male is often a safe bet and the choice of tie or no tie is both a personal one and based on the expectations of others. The higher your reputation, the more you can veer toward your own choice; the less so and I would recommend asking the liaison person where you're a visitor. We can also gain a lot from attending or viewing prior meetings or events, and these are more accessible since online recordings are often available.

What about hair?

While thinking of Geldof's wild hair, featured in the text box overleaf I'm reminded that lack of hair can present a challenge for online speakers who appreciate the value of good lighting. A bald head can shine onscreen, and this could draw unnecessary attention away from your message. Most local pharmacies stock pressed face powder, and this can be used to counter shiny heads or foreheads by patting it with the powder puff provided. Get a colour match by testing it on the skin at the base of your thumb. I have heard of men simply requisitioning their wife's supply!

Otherwise, hair should be neat and not distracting, unless you wish to make a statement with it in your message. It's worth noting that your face needs to be visible to your audience and we subliminally read

Bob Geldof, musician, philanthropist, and keynote speaker, is a good example of appearance authentically embodying the message for his audience. As a musician in the '80s and '90s, Geldof epitomised 'wild' and 'rebellious' for the teenage audience. He was the scruffiest popstar, resplendent in faded denims, messy hair and an unshaven face. His target audience loved his music and his appearance supported it. With support from other musicians, he galvanised support for eliminating hunger in Africa across four decades and because of his authenticity and strong voice, the decision-makers and his supporters accepted his appearance. He has never tried to please his dissenters as far as I can see, and these would be the critics of his appearance. However, one can see that as he aged and began receiving awards such as honorary degrees, freedom of cities and turned his hand to keynote speaking, he often made the decision to don a suit, and even a tie, on occasion. His hair is generally wild, but even that was tamed for his honorary knighthood. His appearance has always supported his message for his chosen audience.

expression as we listen to a speaker. And visible eyes are most important if we want our audience to trust us. If you're being interviewed onscreen and have a side parting with medium to long hair, ensure that you're sitting on the side where most of your face is visible to camera. A few minutes practise and playback or feedback can ensure your appearance is optimised and don't let the interviewer dictate if you're uncomfortable with any aspect of this. One interviewer in America was notorious for putting interviewees, particularly powerful leaders or people he disliked, at a disadvantage by putting them in a comfortable chair with a soft cushion, which threw them back slightly and meant they devoiced.[1] Don't assume the interviewer is on your side!

What about accessories?

Before turning my attention to female attire, it's worth touching on accessories. How many accessories can you afford to wear before they become a distraction to your audience? I was given the magical number of three when I learnt this trade and it's not a bad rule of thumb. You might also find it helpful to watch other speakers and decide if you are distracted by their accessories. If you think three is a good accessory limit and wear glasses and a watch that leaves you with one more accessory. I would caution against accessories that catch the light. Anything which sparkles will, as will large flat metallic pieces, or a watch face. Ensure you practise at that time of day with similar lighting to become aware of the dangers. I had to remove a silver pendant once, minutes before speaking online, as I noticed in the pre-talk chat that it reflected like a mirror in the same lights I needed for professional speaking in the evening. The rule of 'less is more' generally works well for accessories. Don't wear anything you're not prepared to have as a talking point. If your industry is fashion or accessories, that gives you a lot more freedom. I have worked with a wonderful health trainer who goes to every professional event in trainers and colourful fitness wear; her message is loud and clear even before she speaks.

Women in particular

Women's dress code is a big question. If you identify as female, you will be aware of the dilemma we often face. Sadly, women seem to be judged more harshly for their appearance by both men and women and the media lead the way on this. Apart from Place mentioned earlier, I draw on the acronym KISS, Keep It Super-Simple[2]. Dress comfortably and elegantly and err on the side of formality if you have any doubts. Ideally, you want your audience to remember your message and how you embodied it, not something distracting about your appearance. The best actors inhabit their role; the same can be said of the best speakers.

What about make-up?

I've mentioned face powder. It's worth mentioning make-up in general for stage or screen appearances. Anyone who has taken part in amateur dramatics or school plays may have learnt that stage lights drain colour; make-up is therefore worn by all actors. It should simply restore the colour that is drained by the lights and add some additional emphasis to compensate for the distance between actor and audience. Much of the presentation requirements we do in business does not necessitate wearing additional make up unless it takes place on a large stage with professional lighting or under studio lighting on a television set. On those occasions, there are generally professionals on hand to help. In the absence of make-up artists, a balanced approach is required. As we're likely to be speaking with people before and after our stage or screen appearance, looking as natural as possible is important.

In the 21st century, we are highly influenced by a celebrity culture and I'm not a fan of how this has influenced trends in women's make-up. Heavy black eyeliner and thick drawn-on eyebrows add wonderful drama and emphasis to the face of a performer hundreds of meters away in a large arena or projected onto a big screen. However, I believe make-up outside of that setting should enhance the appearance of a person's looks and not draw attention to the make-up itself. Eye contact and facial expression is a vital part of communicating effectively and if this is hidden behind layers of make-up, it can be a barrier. It also distracts from our unique appearance and authentic selves, which can be a deliberate decision. There is no judgement here; just note the decision comes at a cost to potential audience engagement.

Here are a few tips I learnt along the way and on a course with London School of Fashion-trained Sue Robb-King.

'St' indicates stage, 'Sc' indicates screen; S indicates both and G indicates in general.

- St: pink dots on the inner part of your eyes makes them look further away.
- S: pink eye shadow on white skin makes eyes look sore.
- G: black mascara should be avoided unless you've got black hair, an olive complexion or darker. Brown or dark brown is more enhancing.

- G: Investing in good brushes and applicators is more important than expensive make-up.
- G: Get a good skin colour match.
- G: Emulsifying cream is a great inexpensive way for removing makeup.
- Sc: If you wear glasses, you can get away with just lip liner and a medium to dark lipstick for online meetings.

Chapter 15

What Processes of Speech Preparation will Aid my Confidence?

The process of planning

Once you've established the overarching purpose of the public speaking opportunity, I recommend creating a checklist to cater for expectations and eventualities on the day for people, place and space.

However, I would like to devote some time here to planning your content.

What are you going to say?

Ideally, you have been chosen to speak or be interviewed because you are the best person for the role: a subject matter or technical expert perhaps. But what is the purpose of your communication?

Returning again to the Stephen R. Covey principle, 'begin with the end in mind', it applies well to the planning process. After making note of the title, theme or question, establish the purpose by asking this question:

What do I want people to think, feel and/or do as a result of what I say?

The answer will inform your entire speech or the research for your interview. Unless you are averse to writing and find typing on a computer more effective, write down your answer, and keep checking in with the question until you're sure you've thought of everything possible, until the answer is, 'nothing more'.

Now, what do you have to tell, show and demonstrate to people in order to accomplish this? Write it down. This can be a mind map, bullet points or long hand. I like to use pencil so I can rub out and revise easily. Space your ideas out so you can easily add more in without it being cluttered. Colour can be useful to organise points or ideas.

One of your answers to the question above may be to have confidence in what you're saying. Research is therefore essential, and I have a rule of thumb to know about four times more about the subject than I need to deliver, or to allow four hours input for every hour of output for new training or delivery. Putting in the time and effort at this point will ensure confident delivery, including the ability to respond confidently to a question with, 'I don't know but I can find out', knowing adequate preparation has been done. Another good response can be, 'I don't know but if there's someone in the room who does, can I invite them to share their knowledge with us?'

The next stage in planning is organising your speech or presentation. In an interview, this is not possible outside of a presentation which may be required. Interview Preparation is dealt with in Section Five.

To keep within the scope of this book, I'm going to share a tried and trusted outline and write about organising your speech around that. If you want something more elaborate, you can vary this and experiment and explore further. But if you can master this basic outline, you will be better able to grow from a place of confidence. The outline can be likened to a hamburger – a bun with three fillings:

1. First or main point
2. Second point or development
3. Third point or supporting evidence

Much like a hamburger, I would recommend starting with the bun top or your conclusion first, in keeping with the principle of 'begin with the end in mind'. This is your destination, where you will land your speech. So, what will help you to get there? Introduce your subject, expand on it with three points and you should be able to get there in an interesting and informative manner for your audience.

If this idea doesn't appeal to you, here's another approach.

- Read through all your notes then walk away.
- Speak aloud what it's about in no more than five sentences.
- Now repeat this in three sentences.
- Finally, tell the wall, the sky or a listener, in one sentence, what your message is.

I believe this is an essential process because if you can't do this, how easy will it be for your audience to follow you?

You now have the bones of your speech. Fill them out with the meat of your research, taking care to give enough information to support your message. As you go back over it a third time, you will add flesh, the finishing touches, which may reveal that some more meat needs to be added or taken away. As you do, you may note a picture, key word or statistic that will add value for your audience. If using a slide show, make a note of what this might entail, or highlight the word or phrase. This may involve including a different prop; note it down.

You're now in a position to 'try out' your talk. I recommend a run through once without props, so that you can experience the flow of your presentation. Speak it aloud. This is vital as I've written previously, as we use additional parts of our brain and body when we read in our head than when we speak aloud. And this material is going to be delivered vocally so that is what you're practising as well as content. We also need to form the words and sentences and hear it as it fills the air.

Make any necessary adjustments and then add your props. For many people this will mean the use of PowerPoint or similar slide show package. However, if you have a short talk, up to 20 minutes, you may decide not to. Don't ever feel obliged to use slides. Contrary to popular belief, an audience can sustain attention for this period of time – if the speaker is sufficiently engaging. There are now millions of TED talks[1] which prove this to be true.

Managing time

How far in advance you begin preparing a talk and how much time you spend on it are very much dependent on your experience as a speaker and the quantity of research required. In my experience, there are four types of speakers when it comes to time. It's up to you what type of speaker you want to become, so I've written my experience of each to help you decide. Your type will show up in some way, shape or form to an audience, and even if you get pats on the back and told 'that was great', I believe there's only one authentic type. The four are:

1. Wingers – those who 'wing it' and spend very little time preparing.
2. Pretenders – those who pretend they spend very little time preparing.
3. Over-preparers – those who spend hours upon hours of preparing, questionably too many.
4. Respecters – those who put in a significant amount of time preparing for their audience.

I will speak of each one briefly and then focus on the method I recommend.

Wingers. These are people who 'know their stuff'. They are confident, perhaps overconfident, and always do well with sharing their knowledge in meetings. Can you think of one or two that you know? If they are asked to do a presentation or contribute five minutes or less, they do well, although they don't usually manage their time well because they don't have a good sense of how long they've been speaking.

The real problem with wingers is when they are required to do more: a longer presentation or talk or speak at a different venue or to an unfamiliar audience. When the requirement is ten minutes or more, they tend to waffle and there is no clear structure to their talk. They often make a joke about some aspect of their talk and may apologise in advance for something about their delivery, perhaps asking to be prompted when they're time is up, or they'll run over time. A discerning audience member can spot a certain amount of bluff in them. They rely quite a bit on the good grace and mercy of their audience.

A new venue and audience really bring out the weaknesses. I've experienced quite a few Wingers over the years, none of whom are paying for the training themselves. Some can get quite stressed in a new venue as they haven't taken the time to do a tech check or haven't organised the props they need. In one training session, a Winger was rushing around asking to use the visual aids of other presenters. Because of the confidence they had gained (some of whom were over-preparers) they had the self-assurance to say no, knowing it would impact their presentation. That was an interesting learning curve to witness. The old adage 'those who fail to plan, plan to fail' comes to mind. Planning takes time and effort.

The challenge with a new audience for Wingers is that they are exposed. There is no team or ally to fall back on for help or support, and so anything they have left to chance relies on their ability to sort it out in the time they are there. And an audience who have given up their time to listen, rightly expect that time to be worthwhile. If the speaker runs over, we can be intolerant. Even if we are polite or easy going; it is rude to take advantage of that. In my opinion though, the biggest sin Wingers commit is what they do to other speakers when they run over (they seldom underrun in their time because of padding and waffling). If two or more people in a meeting or an event are asked to speak and the first one overruns, it's stressful for the next speaker. The waiting is challenging enough, but while they're waiting, they're wondering if they now need to cut their message short, or question how this will impact the audience.

In fairness, Wingers don't last long in the speaker and presenting space. Eventually, they will be found out, or the stress will persuade them to change their style.

Chapter 15

Hopefully, you now believe that winging it is not an option.

Pretenders. Not a lot has to be said about this group. I include them because they need to be considered for the illusion they create for others and the damage that potentially causes. They will be no problem when it comes to time management when they speak; they have prepared and will keep to time. But when they say they spent a couple of hours preparing, they are at best, forgetful and have others ensuring everything is in place for them or at worst they are braggards, presenting the illusion that their good presentation is down to their natural brilliance.

Very experienced speakers can get away with spending less time on a familiar presentation in a familiar venue, but if the audience is the same, surely they are repeating themselves? If it's a different audience, the presentation should be reworked with that audience in mind. That takes time.

My advice: don't listen to people who dismiss preparation time. Preparation times enormously increases the chances of a good speaking experience. And if something does go wrong, at least you know you have done your best.

Over-preparers. Over-preparers often compensate for their lack of confidence in public speaking with a conviction that if they put lots of time into preparing and practising, they will be fine. Sadly, effort in one area does not guarantee results in another. In fact, the stress of over-preparing can mean exhaustion on the day and a disconnection with the audience that reduces the impact of their message. Another issue can be having too much information and rushing delivery to fit it all in, leaving the audience behind.

This book will be very helpful for over-preparers because you can now spend time acquiring the tools and techniques for confident delivery and can hopefully realise that spending enough time preparing relevant content will lead to easeful delivery, knowing that you're delivering the right message in the right amount of time.

Respecters. Respecters are the people you love to listen to when they share their message. They are calm, even if they're excited. They are considerate and measured in their delivery. You can follow everything they are sharing, and they appear to enjoy being there. They are like good drivers: you step into their vehicle knowing you're going to enjoy the ride and arrive safely at your destination.

A respecter has spent enough time understanding their audience and considering what they need to hear in order to prepare the right amount of material and organises it in a way that is meaningful. They always finish in a reasonable amount of time and generally, you wish they could speak for a little bit longer.

You will be a Respecter if you manage your preparation time correctly and practise what you need to say, aloud, so that you know you're respecting the time of others. Consider running to 85-90% of the total time you've been allocated to speak. It will be 10-15% longer when you are in the room because audience engagement changes the dynamic of your communication, and your speech will expand. This happens even when there isn't laughter, applause or comments from the audience. A speech that doesn't have capacity for this will suffer.[2]

If you ever doubt the importance of keeping to time, ask yourself one question: who in the room do I think deserves less time to speak because of me?

Managing time is an essential component in becoming an expert in public speaking. I've never lacked the confidence to speak in public and I have embedded all the techniques to deliver well, but I've never had a good sense of time. The primary reason I will practise is to ensure that time is respected. If everyone overruns by 30 seconds, not uncommon, in a two-minute elevator pitch, it will take 15 minutes longer to get around a room of 30 people: that's 75 minutes instead of an hour in what is often a two-hour meeting! If that's the impact of running over in two minute-slots, imagine the impact in your average meeting where the presenting takes between ten and thirty minutes per person.

No one realistically complains that a talk was too short. It is even applauded to leave an audience wanting more. What if you planned to finish with a little bit of time to spare? Would that be a gift for both you and your audience?

The process of practise

There are many soundbites on the benefits of practise. I'm pleased that 'Practice makes Perfect' changes to 'Practice makes Progress' at some stage in learning. The question of practise when it comes to public speaking is probably in the top five enquiries I receive at events. A popular myth is that it makes one wooden or less spontaneous. Some people experience nervousness when they practise. Often people just want to know how to practise or what is the right amount of practise. I will address each of these in turn.

1. Dispelling the myths regarding practise

Practise does not make you perfect because perfection is subjective and therefore mythical. Public speaking is not an absolute science where 2+2=4. Therefore, there is no measurement or formula which will get you perfection. You need to create your own definition of when your speech, presentation or interview practise will be good enough or ready. What will you start to feel or what will stop happening? Define it for yourself so you will know when you've accomplished it. It might take a bit of trial and error, and feedback from a colleague, friend or family member to ascertain it. The latter will avoid the audience becoming guinea pigs! Following on from the first section in this chapter, if you tend to over-prepare, you should guard against over practising.

Practise certainly makes progress with your knowledge of content and speaking confidence with delivery.

2. What if practise makes you nervous?

Nervous or underconfident speakers generally find that the process of practising can bring on nervousness and the anxiety of speaking begins from the time they open their mouths in practise. Firstly, I encourage you to read aloud for two minutes every day, starting today. This is because you need to desensitise yourself to the sound of your own voice speaking aloud and without interruption or response. We live in an age of interruption and speaking without it can be alarming. To give you an idea of how little reading two minutes lasts, it's about the time it will take you to read the first four paragraphs of *Respecters* above.

Secondly, visit or revisit Section Two, where the process of doing the Rondo Sequence, which includes breathing and relaxation, should calm those butterflies and have them flying in formation.

Believe me, if you master practising without nerves, you are on your way to mastering speaking without nerves. However, you do need to reframe that which you are calling nerves, and for this I will draw on a wonderful anecdote by Simon Sinek.

Reframing nerves as excitement.[3]

Sinek tells of watching the athletes competing in the London 2012 Olympics as they were interviewed by journalists. As they were asked repeatedly, "Are your nervous?" and they replied with variations of, "No, I'm excited!" he had a realisation. One of the reasons these elite athletes were winners is because they were reframing the negative into a positive.

The same chemical, adrenaline, is released into the body when we're excited as when we're frightened. Biologically, it's there to protect us and give us fuel for an appropriate reaction. The negative framing of calling this release 'nerves' might lead to fright, flight, freeze or fainting where public speaking is concerned. But if we reframe the chemical release as excitement, it can be the rocket fuel that helps us fight, flourish or fly! We can fight our demons and speak brilliantly, flourish as we embrace the energy that will give our words feeling that connects us to our audience and enables us to fly high in our speaking opportunities – all because we are loving instead of loathing that adrenaline.

Chapter 15

Case study: Hugh and Alice[4]

Most people can conquer fear of public speaking. Of all the people I've worked with in over two decades, there have been two exceptions: one in private coaching and the other in group training. As I've stated previously, there is no such thing as a bad voice, only a voice with barriers to public speaking, physical and psychological. Within the remit of this book and in terms of my training as a coach, I can work with barriers to a certain degree. In fact, sometimes, equipping learners with communication tools and techniques give the level of confidence that eliminates some psychological barriers too. But occasionally wounds run too deep for this. As a result, some people will decide never to put themselves in the way of danger and not even reach out to engage with a voice and speech coach to help. You may be at the next stage, where you have bought this book because you've decided to master this fear. Having made use of counselling and therapy myself, I would encourage you to consider talking to a professional, should reading and applying this book's techniques still leave you terrified. I have had initial conversations with a few people seeking help and they have realised they need to deal with some demons first. This is courageous and I applaud their wisdom. I would never make that recommendation but will help people recognise that I can't meet their public speaking needs at this point.

The two clients who got past this stage were Hugh and Alice. Hugh worked with me across two years to acquire every tool and technique I had developed at the time. He still hated doing the public speaking gigs he was required to do for his organisation. A medium-sized charity, there was no one better than him to speak because he had been there since the start, knew everything there was to know, and was passionate about the service they offered. But every time he had an upcoming gig, he felt sick to his stomach with nerves in the lead up to the talk and during it. He did not want to explore the reasons for this, which I knew from a throwaway remark, lay in a difficult childhood. Following the talk which I indicated would be the final outcome assessment talk, having done everything to prepare him, he came to our next session with his solution: he had gone to his doctor and had beta blockers to take for subsequent presentations. They absolutely helped and he was able to move on.

I'm not someone who would suggest drugs as a solution to anyone, but because a positive experience can fuel confidence, even if it is enhanced by medication, I am making this information known to you.

That is what happened with Alice.

She was part of a training course that took place over several months, dealing with a broad variety of soft skills training, including presentation skills. When she came to me quietly to explain her situation, I recognised that she was in a similar state of mind as Hugh. I had seen her present competently, but knew it was agony for her. Having explained that individual work with a voice and speech coach or a counsellor was the best solution, I shared Hugh's solution. In the final session, she came to me, happier and more confident, sharing how much the beta blockers had helped.

They are a stop gap, not a solution, and I would urge you to exhaust other solutions first and to see them for the temporary assistant they are. Hugh has since trained other people to do the talks and Alice is still training.

3. How do I practise?

This is the million-dollar question, and I hope my fool-proof process will act as a base point for a five- to twenty-minute speech. I suggest you then redesign it to work best for you and adapt it for situations where you don't have the luxury to be this thorough. Although this is a base for an inexperienced speaker, I know that if I follow this process, I'm guaranteed greater confidence and success when I speak. Feedback from clients has been similarly positive.

Stage 1: Spend time planning your talk, as outlined in the planning stage above.

Stage 2: Create and select slides or other props to enhance your content.

Stage 3, Practise 1: practise it aloud and adjust until it's the right time length, delivered according to the modulation guidelines in Chapter 11. It may be that you can't decide what to leave out if the time is still over, at which point ask your feedback person for guidance on what to drop in advance of Practise 2.

Stage 4, Practise 2: Deliver it for a colleague, friend, family member or coach, preferably timing it and perhaps recording your voice. Listen to their feedback and make notes.

Stage 5: Apply the changes you agree with. (Optional) Practise 3: Deliver it to get the timing right again.

Stage 6, Practise 3/4: Deliver it to the same person again.

Stage 7: When you are satisfied with the content and initial delivery, make prompt cards if you're using them. Before you do, follow these instructions:

- How can you sum up what you're speaking about in five sentences?
- Condense that into three sentences.
- What are the three most important words?
- What is the most important word to describe your message? This could be different to any of the three previous words as it may be the theme, topic or purpose.

If you can nail this, you may be able to put less on a prompt card or cards, and you will know that if all else fails, you can expand on what you've spoken or written above.

Stage 8, Practise 5-9: Speak it until it flows with minimal reference to the notes. Do not read from the slides.

You may wish to adopt a memorisation technique at this point, especially if you have decided not you use notes. A popular one, dating back to ancient Rome and Greece, is called the method of loci. It consists of memorising your talk as a visual journey around a room or a place and assigning a part of your talk there. As long as it alternates with making meaningful eye contact with your audience, it is a sound technique, worth trying. It will appeal more to strongly visual learners.

Stage 9, Final practise: This should be a day before your talk, preferably not in the evening as a rested brain after a good night's sleep will work in your favour on the day. Note that even if you feel your talk lacks lustre, the energy of being in front of your audience will revitalise it. Remind yourself that it's their first time hearing it; they won't know what has been left out or added.

If you are delivering a training course or have a weekly presentation, this process is not sustainable or realistic. For a course, try it for practising a portion at a time, delivering an overview, or focus on the parts you feel less confident about.

With a weekly presentation, invest in this process once and then learn from the feedback for the next one. Reduce it as your confidence grows. Always invite feedback from a trusted meeting attendee and be specific in one area each time. Here are three key questions you could ask:

- How did you experience my presentation?
- What went well?
- What could I have done better?[5]

4. What is the right amount of practise?

This is, as you may have guessed, the how-long-is-a-piece-of-string question! From the process of practise above, you'll have some idea of the maximum of practises you need to have. Multiply this by the length of the delivery. Ten hours for a five- to twenty-minute talk is not uncommon. I've heard of people, under the guidance of organisers, putting in a hundred hours of practise for an 18-minute TED talk. They are flawless and it looks effortless for a reason.

You will know when you've practised too little because when you deliver it in your meeting or on stage, you may lose your place, be thrown by a curveball, feel anxious about it going wrong, and most importantly, you won't be fully engaged with your audience.

You will know when you've practised enough, when you've done your presentation and the delivery has gone well. Repeat that quantity of practise a couple more times before you drop practise time, and only then if you feel you can afford to. I love the well-known quote "the more I practice, the luckier I get,"[6] and this applies to public speaking as much as it does to golf and shooting a gun.

Practising your talk again and again to manage nervousness is not a solution; practise reframing, breathing and relaxation instead. There are techniques and tools in Section Two and additional ones in Appendix 1.

When you've practised enough, it is still possible to lose your train of thought. But you'll be more relaxed about getting back on track because your content will be emblazoned across your mind, or you'll know exactly where to refer to in your notes. There will almost certainly be curveballs, but you should be able to handle them because your practise is embedded. Most importantly, you will know that your practise has been your greatest gift to you audience because you have the joy of fully engaging with them as you embody the message you deliver.

Chapter 16

What Are the Best Tools For The Job Online?

Up to March 2020, most leaders didn't have to think about speaking online much. The COVID-19 pandemic changed the way we meet forever. Telephone conferencing was popular for international and corporates, and Skype, Microsoft Teams, and Zoom were available but under-utilised in most industries. We travelled or worked local.

That seems like history as I write, as the pandemic accelerated our use of online meeting and event facilitation in an unprecedented manner. We are also facing a climate crisis where excessive travelling is no longer considered acceptable by many organisations and countries. A mixture of in-person, hybrid and online meetings and presentations is increasingly normal, and this is appropriate for our global village. This is unlikely to change as our reach expands globally and nationally with geography no longer a criterion to finding a 'good fit' for suppliers, employees, colleagues and clients. New generations of speakers coming up will never know a time when meeting online was the exception rather than the rule.

As people from all walks of life have adapted to some form of online technology, my focus in this chapter will be to share insights for effective engagement and offer you techniques to improve your online presence. My experience is that those attending meetings do what is necessary for showing up. This is not enough for current or aspiring speakers and presenters. I will endeavour to equip you to make the audience's experience more engaging and give you confidence that you're connecting well with the audience.

Speaking to a camera

For most of our working lives, speaking to a camera was at best a choice. Now, people who would never put themselves in front of a camera are obliged to do so, and the difference between those who can and those who can't do it well has become clear. As with all the skills I help develop, nothing about speaking to camera is difficult, it's just difficult when you don't know how. Few of us older than Millennials have been equipped for this as part of our education or work.

The techniques here will help you speak to an audience via camera. In several ways, there's little difference to speaking to a camera and in person. It's still important to deliver your message with power, clarity and confidence. But even confident speakers can freeze or burn when faced with a camera. Talking to a piece of equipment is not natural; but with technique and practise, you can make it look like it is.

Your rectangle – optimal position for meetings

In Chapter Four, I took you through the seated posture. When you're in front of a camera on an online platform, that point just above eye-level should be your camera. Ideally, I would recommend you adjust your desk and screen height if it's not. It might be worth considering purchasing an external camera if my recommendation compromises how you use your screen for day-to-day work.

The next step is to adjust the angle of your screen so that your eyes are in the top one third. If you look at the images in Fig 6, the picture on the left shows how many people show up on screen. As with photography, amateurs tend to set their eyes as the mid-point in the lens. The result is that we are not only giving people more of the room but denying them some of ourselves. They're without your presence in

Fig. 6.1 and 6.2 – Can you see how the image on the right shows more presence than the image on the left. And which offers more distraction?

the room already, so give them as much as you can onscreen. More of you means that your gestures are more likely to be visible too. If you are participating in a way that means your gestures matter, sit further back than you need to for general keyboard use. This means that looking at faces onscreen and looking in the camera are more subtle as less eye movement is required.

When you attend your next online meeting, observe how everyone else is presenting themselves onscreen. What impact does it have on your ability to effectively engage and connect with them?

Let me suggest that you do this without harsh criticism. I believe it's important to show up with an attitude of compassion, humility and generosity - to be kind when looking at others. But there are simple ways to make the most of what you've got.

Position for presenting

Your position for presenting online will largely depend on what the presentation requirements are. It's easy to slip into the habit of presenting sitting down because it seems easier and you think everyone can see you on the screen, so why stand up?

In a word – energy.

It's challenging to communicate with energy sitting down, although the techniques I provided in Section Two demonstrates that it's possible. Lack of energy isn't as much of an issue for a smaller group and a more intimate setting but consider what will work best for your audience and adjust accordingly. I also understand that for some, your PC does not adjust from sitting to standing and raising the screen may be a challenge. Perhaps your space doesn't allow you to move back much but do everything you can to maximise your audience experience. Depending on how far you want to go in presenting professionally, you may consider investing in equipment that raises your game. If your organisation doesn't consider supporting this, hopefully the standard is equitable. It's always worth having that conversation though.

> As a member of a professional speaking organisation, I heard a huge variety of advice and recommendations filling up our social media feeds on how to overcome challenges of speaking online at the start of 2020. The technophiles rushed to spend money on equipment, and this was reflected in the cost of online meeting equipment soaring. Your body and voice are still your best two pieces of equipment! My favourite tips were about using everyday objects at home to 'make it work'. Coming in at #1 was using an ironing board and laundry basket to raise the height of a laptop or screen so that one could present standing. It works, and your audience can't see the set-up! I've been known to use a recipe stand for my notes too.

Plan place

Once you've got your screen position sorted, it's time to switch on the camera and check out what your audience are seeing. This falls into two categories: you and your space or background.

I dealt with 'the hair and make-up of presenting' in Chapter 14. For online presenting, focus on your purpose in being online or on camera. If you're working towards a promotion, acquiring a new client or position, your standards need to be high. But any professional meeting needs to communicate your commitment to your profession. Now, translate that to a 'camera ready' appearance.

What is behind you in the rectangle the audience can see? If you are embodying the message and wish to maximise engagement with the audience, this space needs to be uncluttered. What will enhance your message? What will distract? While it's optional to blur your background or use a green screen to create your ideal background, your lighting has to be very good to avoid an odd 'halo' effect and some hairstyles can make this even more of a challenge. Unless you fill most of the screen, a blank wall can be a little dull. Use your experience of other meetings to guide you as to what helps you focus most on the speaker's message.

Good lighting is very important.[1] A window or light behind you will throw you into silhouette, making it difficult for your audience to engage with you. Ideally, have good light coming from in front and above you, but take care of position if you wear glasses as this will reflect in them and reduce engagement with your audience as well as providing distraction. Consider the light at the time of day when you're presenting, ensuring you practise at least once to the camera at that time. Don't use florescent lights not designed for camera as they will flicker. Apart from the energy factor of low voltage, it's also cooler. Too much, or hot lighting can see you glow or drip in front of the camera as a sweat breaks out – not pretty or pleasant for you especially.

Sound quality is another important consideration. A sound check function is available on every online platform and if you're presenting, meet with the organiser for a sound check at least fifteen minutes before others are admitted. Fortunately, people are much better at letting you know if they can't hear you properly than if your lighting is poor. It's essential to have enough bandwidth connection for your call too, so that your sound doesn't break up. It's tricky to sort these out once the meeting has started and, apart from being potentially annoying for your audience, you give a poor first impression. Finally on sound, most laptops and computers have adequate microphones for meeting participation if you're seated at your desk for a meeting. However, if you're a speaker and particularly if you're standing, you will need additional amplification. There are beautiful microphones out there, but for less than £50, a Rode lapel mic[2] produces quality sound. I chose one that is not remote because it is less likely to pick up interference from other electronic equipment. A disadvantage is that I need to remember to clip it back on my lapel if I leave my desk in the course of a meeting!

Other online tools that are fit for purpose

You can spend a fortune on tools and gadgets for online speaking and they go in and out of fashion and stock. I will just mention two I've used and leave you to find gadget experts for the rest. **Green screens** were considered essential in the first year of lockdown amongst speakers, and my artificial office background complete with logo was voted best background at one PSA meeting I attended, yet natural backgrounds became more popular as we entered year two and our third lockdown in the UK. Zoom fatigue was associated with the visual interference created by all but the most professional set-ups. You need to spend a good deal of money on lighting so that backgrounds don't have static edges or disappearing body parts! It's also become clear that people find identifiably artificial backgrounds less authentic; it's up to you to decide what aligns with your personal branding and core values. It made a significant difference for one client who started his own business from a caravan on his driveway. He was able to project a professional image that aligned with the quality of his work when he set up an office background with a company logo. In conclusion, only use a Green Screen if you can present a more professional image than not using one.

My favourite editing tool for my online videos has been **Video Cutter Expert**. I like it because it's simple to use and it's free. If you apply the principles of good public speaking on modulation[3], you will have opportunities to edit videos to a decent standard. Sharing your expertise via online video is an excellent way to engage your target audience and make an impression.

Meeting management

If you are facilitating an online meeting as part of your role, this is a public speaking opportunity that requires additional skills. It's essential that you are familiar with the workings of your online platform so that you can admit people and engage with everyone in the virtual room with ease. Most platforms have a waiting room or foyer so that you can ensure the attendees have all been invited; I consider this an essential feature to use after one meeting I attended was 'Zoom bombed'. For good meeting facilitation, I would recommend prearranging a co-host who is happy to admit people and keep an eye on the chat facility. A good host cannot multitask effectively with people and technology and people are happy to help. If it's a paid webinar and you don't have a staff member or a colleague you can ask, discounted or free entry is often an adequate 'thank you'.

A wonderful blessing and challenge of online meetings is that they are booked for a specific end as well as start time. This means that if you're facilitating, you need to honour that time. It's far easier for people to drop an apology in the chat and leave for their next meeting in an online setting than stand up and walk out of a physical room. As more meetings are taking place online, since remote working became normalised, it's essential in a professional environment to have an agreed agenda before you begin. I suggest sending it out at least 48 hours before and framing your agenda items as questions. This will ensure that you have engagement from the time people read it. I've supplied a sample below to give you an idea of what this might look like, using an average company's monthly meeting agenda as an example:

Traditional Meeting Agenda	Timings	Thinking Environment Meeting Agenda
1. Company Management Updates	10:00	(Opening Round) What's New? Who's New?
2. Sales Report	10:20	How are our Sales doing against Quarterly Forecasts? What Factors are at Play?
3. Financial Report	10:40	How are our finances? What would you like to know?
4. HR Report	11:00	How are you all doing? What do you need to know?
5. A.O.B.	11:20	What else do we need to consider? Over to you? (Closing Round)
6. DONM	11:40	Confirmation of next meeting and Close

This then provides a template for your Minutes with the additional columns to the right of 'Who?' and 'By when'. This will facilitate accountability within a timeframe. Remember to honour the time. *If you run over, you are making a conscious choice that the next person delivering is less worthy of the time.* The planning stage is the time to revise the meeting timings. Confirm the allocated time in your covering email; that is the time to agree and commit. Lack of consideration of the time and voice of others by senior leaders is an issue I've picked up as I've listened to middle managers in training. It impacts the quality of the meeting and the quality of the information.

After the meeting

If you're presenting in a meeting, your public speaking opportunity will be further enhanced if your follow up is of a high standard. This applies to delivering a talk, online training, or webinars. It's important to follow up on any commitments you've made, so do make a note of these as you go. If it's additional to your planned follow-up, pausing to do this will be excused by your audience, or ask your producer/co-host to make a note in advance. This may include handouts or links to information that will enhance the audience's engagement with the topic. I tend not to provide handouts in advance unless registration has revealed learners who depend on visual aids to engage or it's an essential part of the learning process. This is because I want my audience to be present and engaged in the moment, relying on their brains to remember what is salient for them. If meeting or training organisers request this, I ensure it's for a good reason, otherwise, I'm happy to provide it to the organisers or attendees in follow up material. A feedback form is something I like to include for development purposes and to allow the conversation to continue. More details and suggestions on feedback is provided later.

If you are being paid to present or train online, it is advisable to have a backup plan should the technology or power fail. For this reason, record and send your final practise to the organisers. You may choose to send them the handouts or other supporting material to distribute under these circumstances. A signed contract and payment or part payment in advance ensure that your Intellectual Property is protected.

If your commitment to public speaking requires facilitating a business meeting, a rotating Chair and Secretary/Minute Taker who can populate the Minutes template as you go, will be an advantage. Making these rotating positions is a great way to develop both discipline and empathy amongst leaders. If at all possible, send the minutes within an hour of the meeting and no later than 24 hours to ensure optimal engagement.

Some of these ideas are clearly transferable to meetings in person. Apply what works for you in engaging with your audience and putting them first.

A note about voiceover work

In closing, you may be interested in doing voiceover work. This has very specific requirements for the standard of soundproofing and quality of equipment required. The organisations who offer work in this area will provide you with the requirements and you will be asked to send through a sample of your work.

Not only are they interested in your voice, but they will rate you on the quality and consistency of the sound you can produce. I collaborate with people who do voiceovers and one amusing tip I can offer is that setting up an ironing board with a duvet over it acts as a great soundscape!

Personally, I would struggle with breathing and posture. The costs of setting up a good sustainable space may not bring adequate returns on your investment. Have conversations with people who are already doing voiceover work, as part of your decision-making process.

Chapter 17
What Tools do I Need for In-Person and Hybrid Presentations?

Presenting in person

How exciting if you've received an invitation to present in person, whether it's an interview, a talk, a meeting or training delivery! This is what you've been preparing for and your probable reason for purchasing this book. Presenting in person should be a wonderful experience and now that you've come this far, it's time to consider what tools you need for this stage in the process. Whatever the invitation, you need to be organised.

A checklist is your best friend for any event. Create your own and add to this anything the organiser or meeting host has requested. Tick it off as you set it aside the night before or next morning and place them with the shoes you will be wearing. It's unlikely you will leave the house in your socks or bare feet! **Notes** are a very reassuring companion, even if you don't intend to use them.

- For any presentation using slides, you will need to bring your charged **laptop** and a **power cable**. Even if I've been asked to email the presentation in advance to be displayed on their software, my laptop is reassuring to have in case of issues with the venue or software compatibility.

- **A clicker**, formally known as a Presenter Wireless Remote Control, that you will have practised with. It ensures that you can make eye contact with your audience and don't compromise your posture or visibility during a presentation.
- **Speakers**, if I am playing any videos or audio through my laptop.
- **An HDMI cable**, for connecting to a screen. I also have a VGA cable, but these are mostly obsolete now. Check with the venue as to what's required. Even if they have an HDMI cable, these often disappear from venues, so I don't leave anything to chance. And label your cables brightly so you don't leave any behind.
- **A phone charger**, I keep a spare one with a spare laptop power cable with my kit so that I'm never caught short. My phone will be on silent or airplane mode during meetings.
- **Handouts** and/or **feedback forms**, should be printed and packed in a plastic folder in good time. You don't want to find out the night before that you have run out of printer paper or ink!
- **Props** should be placed together in a suitable container.
- **Treats** to guard against a rumbling tummy but also to use as a fun prize for audience participation. Careful not to hit anyone if you throw them, though, which I have been known to do!

For training, highlight all the trainer material needed for that training in the manual or notes, and set them aside the day before. This is in addition to baseline kit which includes:

- **Training manual** – mine and the participants
- **Stationery** – including pens, pencils with built in erasers, highlighters, post-it notes, stationery holders for each table
- **A clear storage box** – to keep my kit in one place between sessions
- **A suitcase on wheels** - to transport everything.

Arrive in plenty of time to ensure that your equipment works. Introduce yourself at the venue reception and give positive feedback when appropriate. I've had fantastic service as a result of this and it means that when there is a problem, people go out of their way to help.

Accommodation and venue

Across several years of training and keynote speaking, I've learnt much by making mistakes or assumptions. I hope you can avoid some of these with the following considerations.

- Always check with the accommodation that they have your booking, and it has your requirements. Personally, I like to have a bath after a day on my feet training and this is not a given for all accommodation
- Check with the venue that they are expecting you and that all is going according to plan
- Ensure you have the right address for both, as especially for hotels, cities often have more than one hotel from the same hotel group
- Check with both that GPS will take you to the right entrance and if you need parking, find out where that is and any restrictions or regulations. Read the website and reviews as often employees don't have the issues occasional travellers do. Checking their Google My Business page can be really helpful if you have doubts
- Check with the venues if they're aware of any major events happening on the date or dates of your event, as this will impact traffic and parking
- Ensure you've checked timings with Google Maps for the time and day you're travelling
- For speaking or training venues, I like to find out if there's a café open nearby in case I arrive too early at a venue with no facilities, or my arrival would inconvenience them
- If you're staying overnight, it might be worth bringing your own pillow. There is one hotel chain I won't use because I find

the beds too hard and the pillows too firm. That may give the impression of 'The Princess and the Pea' story, but training on a bad night's sleep is an experience I never wish to repeat.

What changes for a hybrid presentation?

This was a new experience for many of us from 2021 and it's been a delightful challenge. I don't manage the technical parts, leaving that to experts in the field, but it has provided a wonderful opportunity for people to participate online, if being present would pose a challenge.

The number one rule is the same as for a presentation: be inclusive.

Ensure that your presentation includes everything that is required for people in the room and online, adjusting your language and materials to include both. The previous chapter deals with online tools and techniques. Sometimes, hybrid can mean that the material will be streamed at a later date, so it is important to acknowledge that. An example of a welcome I do with one group goes something like this,

'A warm welcome to everyone, here especially those joining us online today or if you're watching this later.'

If you haven't been provided with the information in advance, check with the Tech Support as to who and how many have registered online so that you can greet them and introduce them as a group to the room. Having checked where the camera or cameras are, you then treat each camera as an additional person in the room, making eye contact as often as you do with any person or table in the room.

What do the audience need – before, during and after?

If you've made a commitment to provide any follow-up material, it's important to do this in a timely manner, perhaps even supplying it to the Tech Support via email or USB to be attached in the chat at the end of the meeting, or available as a PDF to those watching later. If you've planned well, there's no reason why it can't be supplied within 24 hours of the meeting or emailed by the meeting hosts at the end of your talk or meeting.

SECTION FIVE
And What Else?

Chapter 18
Consider Embodying a Thinking Environment©

At this stage, you've read and hopefully learnt a lot about speaking and body language; how to do it, a little about how not to do it, and the peripheral considerations around that. You've also read a little about the other half of communication, namely listening. I opened the book acknowledging that my experience started as an audience member – that's all about listening and watching.

It is my hope that you have picked up on several aspects of listening so far:

- Listening to and tuning into yourself – your heartbeat, your gut, your inner voice
- Listening to and researching the organisers and your clients so that what you're communicating is meeting their needs
- Listening to or tuning in to your audience as you speak
- Listening to feedback.

To further enhance your listening, allow me to share my experience of the coaching framework I use and how it has helped me and my clients in our communication. It's my hope that through reading this, you may consider the benefits and find your best way of showing up in communication from a listening perspective. I've asked many questions throughout; it might be helpful to pause to consider these as you work through the pages.

'The quality of everything we do begins with the quality of the thinking we do first'[1]

When I read *Time to Think* and other books by Nancy Kline, and undertook qualifying courses,[2] it was with the hope of finding a coaching methodology that complemented my work. However, since adopting the components you'll read about below, I've realised that it not only helped me engage with my clients more, but helped both them and me engage in better communication. Considering the quote above, if public speaking is the 'thing' that we do, the quality of our thinking really matters. And if we are expecting our audience to think, feel and do something because we have spoken, the quality of their thinking as they listen really matters. Therefore, facilitating the very best environment for this to take place really does matter.

The Ten Components are ten behaviours that have been identified by Kline to facilitate quality thinking. They are; Attention, Equality, Ease, Appreciation, Encouragement, Feelings, Information, Difference, Incisive Questions™ and Place. Because Nancy expresses it so beautifully herself, I will introduce each one with a quotation from her,[3] explain my experience of it and add an idea or question to help your spoken engagement benefit. You may be able to add more ideas as you consider it in your particular context and seek to incorporate it in your public speaking.

Attention is *listening without interruption* and with *interest in where the person will go next in their thinking; attention is an act of creation.*

Watching and listening to people helps us to know them. When I studied drama, we were taught that there are three ways to understand a character: what they say, what they do and what others say about them. We learn more by listening and watching, than by speaking.

If we are the speaker at an event, that will mean listening to the organiser beforehand, asking good questions, and paying attention to the response. At the event itself, it's taking time to mingle and getting to know something about the audience in advance. Referring to something observed or shared in the lead up to your talk is a powerful engagement tool as it's topical and gives the audience a greater sense of belonging as they listen. Attention helps gauge the mood of the audience too.

> In one of my first training gigs, I picked up in conversation over pre-training coffee that there was much cynicism about the course, fuelled by fear of redundancies. I also gleaned that the energy levels and morale in the room were low due to the impact of strike action in one division of the organisation. I was sensitive to this as I brought my enthusiasm for the learning into the room, acknowledging where they were and what they were going through. It was paid back to me in spades with their engagement levels.

For a networking event, we can glean valuable information that will help our elevator pitch be more relevant. In an interview or meeting, giving the other people in the room our generative attention facilitates better engagement when it is your turn to speak. Generally, I find people who are interested are more interesting.

Nancy recommends looking at people with a gaze that is 'not too fierce' and refrain from nodding as even this can be an interruption. Perhaps try this for your next few meetings or events and note if it enhances the engagement of others. What have you learnt that you may have otherwise missed?

With public speaking opportunities, paying greater attention can help us read the mood of a room during our talk and can help us really hear the questions afterwards. It can help remove assumptions if we are really listening and gives us permission to ask for clarity if we don't fully understand what is being asked.

Chapter 18

What do I notice when I really give my full attention to my audience? What does it cost me and what is the gain?

Equality is *regarding each other as thinking peers, giving equal time to think; even in a hierarchy people can be equal as thinkers.*

Equality can help with audience engagement if we have mistakenly assumed that as the speaker, we must be the expert. Yes, the audience wants to know what we know. The speaker may be the expert and the audience are the potential learners, but in treating the audience as an equal in their thinking, you will have a better sense of how to pace your delivery, when to pause, how much to explain to your listeners and how simple that explanation needs to be. As equal thinkers, you won't tell people what to think; you will tell them enough so they can think for themselves.

Following a talk I delivered on the Ten Components, a cleaning company in the south of England decided to practise this. Every week, the owner had a 30-minute meeting with his staff. In 'Matters Arising', the staff were encouraged to share issues that had arisen, and solutions were encouraged from everyone in the room. Because the staff were treated as equal thinkers, everyone felt able to speak out.

It is often the case that a cleaner will have a better solution to a problem in the field than the manager who stays in the office. If equality wasn't part of their culture, the cleaners would be more likely to hold back in a meeting environment and the business would lose out on insights from people who can add great value.

If I considered that my audience are equal to me in their thinking and I equal in my thinking to them, how will that affect the way I engage with them?

Ease: *Ease creates; urgency destroys.*

We live in a society with a rush hour but no identified 'ease hour'. We work with deadlines and never hear about 'live-lines'. Do we produce our best under pressure, or do we just not know an alternative?

The component of Ease is a favourite discovery of a Thinking Environment© for me. It has been my experience that we do our best thinking in an easeful atmosphere. It follows that we may well do our best speaking when we prepare, practise and deliver our talk in an environment of ease. No matter how fast internet speed becomes, our brain still processes information at the same rate as our great-grandparents. I believe we create a stressful environment if we expect more of our audience.

Have you been to a talk where the speaker has been given ten or 20 minutes and is clearly trying to fit a much longer talk into that time? They speak more quickly, they seem rushed, and it feels a bit like a race. What do we notice? How does our body respond? How much do we learn? Speakers admit that they do this to get all their information out; what they might not realise is that the information might not be going in!

> I once took a call from a prospective client who got in touch because he received feedback from his work that he spoke too quickly. As he shared his story at an alarming rate, I could feel my heartbeat increase and my stress levels rising. When he shared that it also impacted his personal relationships, particularly his marriage, I was not surprised. Although the call could not have lasted more than ten minutes, I was exhausted when I put the phone down. I felt this was a small taste of how stressful an environment devoid of ease can be!

Ease and energy can coexist. I am not advocating slow; a talk should be practised so that it fits easily into the time allowed and editing must take place if it doesn't. If a gathering is told the meeting will end at a certain time, or a speaker will speak for 20 minutes, and the meeting or speaker runs over, they don't know how much longer they will be kept. Will it be two minutes or ten? Does the facilitator or speaker respect people's time? While they are thinking these thoughts, they are not listening to the message.

Chapter 18

Ease creates an atmosphere where good thinking and engagement can flourish. What can you do to make Ease part of your speaking practise?

Appreciation is *noticing what is good and saying it; the human mind works best in the presence of appreciation.*

A speaker who is grateful for the opportunity to speak, whether paid or unpaid, engages better with their audience. Gratitude or appreciation flow out of them and is even better when expressed. As I've written elsewhere, a smile says, 'I'm glad to be here' and expressing appreciation in words sets a wonderful tone for a talk. Even if there have been a few disasters leading up to your opportunity to speak, find something to appreciate, such as people's patience, their presence, the last person to speak or introduce you, even the weather or what you had for lunch. It won't just lift the spirits of your audience; it will lift your spirit too.

> I once delivered a talk at a hotel in Peterborough, where it emerged there was a sewerage problem in the street outside. Acknowledgment of the issue through making jokes and listening to jokes meant that we could appreciate each other's sense of humour and how delightful the training situation had been the day before. We bonded as a group in our suffering!

As our minds work best where there is appreciation, we will better engage our audience. If you are anxious as you prepare for that interview or talk, what can you appreciate about this opportunity? About the audience? About yourself?

Encouragement is *giving courage to go to the unexplored edge of thinking by ceasing competition as thinkers.*

I first heard Brené Brown quote, "Comparison is the thief of joy"[4]. I find that so true. Competition and comparison can mar our pleasure as we prepare to speak, as we sit in a meeting room, event or interview awaiting our turn.

Encouragement is the opposite to this. It's good to share your plan, and practise with a colleague or friend who you know will encourage you. Encouragement means 'to give courage' and courage comes from the French word 'cœur' meaning 'heart'. Take heart about your talk – value the good in it. Encourage others who are speaking or interviewing alongside you. Sometimes, focusing on others and encouraging them can help us to feel encouraged ourselves. When our goal is fulfilling our potential and doing our best, we think better, even to 'the unexplored edges of thinking'. It becomes a more creative process that can benefit us and our organisation more.

Be aware of comparing or competing in a way that may not serve you and your audience. What will encouragement look like for you as you approach your speaking opportunity?

How can your presentation encourage others? How can others take heart from your words? How will that influence how you plan, prepare and deliver your talk?

Feelings is *welcoming the release of emotion.*

This component is easy to justify in relation to effective spoken communication. In Section Two, we discussed connection, how important it is for your breath to connect with your emotional centre. When you're connecting with your breath, it's far more likely that your voice will engage your audience and you'll connect with them on an emotional level. It warms and colours your voice so that people enjoy listening to you more. This is true whether you're talking about something factual such as financial figures or an emotive issue such as world hunger. In fact, money is a highly emotive issue so acknowledging the potential response to financial figures will be empowering.

You also need to welcome the release of emotion in yourself. Your emotional and bodily response to public speaking needs to be recognised and harnessed so that it works for you and not against you.

There is value in considering Feelings as you prepare your talk. What reactions can you expect in response to the information you're sharing? How can your choice of words and delivery influence that for the best possible outcome?

"Emotion trumps reason" is a favourite quote from motivational speaker, Simon Sinek[5]. He uses it in the context of a book about purpose, *Start With Why: How great leaders inspire everyone to take action*, where he states that people do not prioritise rationale in their decision-making. We like to think we do, but our gut reaction is stronger. This applies to both our feelings when we speak and the feelings we stir in our audience.

How can you anticipate and prepare for your feelings and the feelings your talk will engender?

Information is *absorbing the facts (data, social context, denial)*.

As a listener in a Thinking Environment©, we share information when it will help our Thinker think, or to dismantle denial; it is about seeking veracity and maintaining integrity.

Public speaking is about sharing information, usually quite a lot, with an audience, ideally without interruption. It is often followed by an opportunity to ask questions. An audience may challenge the information or request more. Sadly, it can also sometimes be abused by people who feel the need to share their information, perceiving that your audience needs their unsolicited wisdom.

It is therefore important that a speaker selects the information they choose to share, wisely. Often you are asked to speak because you are considered the expert in this field. How will you use your knowledge of the audience to carefully select the right information and the right amount of information? How will you share your knowledge and wisdom to benefit your listeners? How will you interpret it so that it's of maximum benefit? In recent years, there has been a growing appreciation for stories as a medium to share information. You may also wish to use pictures, graphs, props and demonstrations to reinforce that information.

On the subject of information, a recent phenomenon with the unkind moniker of 'mansplaining' has arisen due to a tendency of some men to over-explain something to women because they believe, consciously or subconsciously that they will struggle to understand it otherwise. I would hasten to add that it could equally exist in a context dominated by women where a man feels patronised, although I haven't heard examples of this personally.

The issue is that this is done across the board where speakers perceive their audience to be considerably less intelligent than themselves. I raise this as a cautionary note. Be careful of over-explaining anything to your audience, they may feel insulted by it. A good speaker makes you feel intelligent while you're learning, not stupid, or patronised. Examine your assumptions in the preparation stage and seek to find one good example.

What information will you choose to share with your audience and what is its value?

Difference is *championing our inherent diversity of identity and thought.*

The component of appreciating Difference is about believing that diversity in thinking improves the thinking in the room. Our differences help us to think better together. If you think about herd instinct or 'yes-men', you can appreciate that difference in thinking is better than sameness.

When we are speaking in public, we will engage better with our audience if we assume that we are different and that we think differently to each other. This is something to celebrate, rather than something to fear because the opportunity to learn and to ignite thinking is much greater. Most of our freshest thinking comes from people who are different to us, so when we can address an audience who are quite different to us, we have the potential to accomplish so much more with the sharing of our ideas.

At the end of the day, which would you prefer: to speak to a group of people who will nod their head in agreement with potentially no buy in, or having some people challenge your thinking and provide an opportunity for you to go deeper and win them over? What do you think the audience would find more interesting?

How will you plan and prepare your talk, knowing that people think differently to you? How will you prepare if you know people might disagree with you? How can you embrace that?

Incisive Questions™ *free the human mind of untrue assumptions lived as true.*

Let me begin by acknowledging that Incisive Questions™ is a big ask and potentially beyond the scope of many talks. They are questions which allow the thinker to play with an idea based on a true and liberating assumption *they* have identified. But it's possible if you are speaking, for instance, to an audience of scientists who have just discovered something about physics that now liberates them from previously held assumptions. In a Time to Think session, the asking of an incisive question usually comes towards the end. An example might be where a client has removed the assumptions around his value to his manager and his chances of promotion. An incisive question might be "If you knew that your manager considers you worth promoting, what would you do next?" It can often be an if/then question, which puts it in the realm of possible questions you might want your audience to contemplate. It is beautifully playful and stimulates the thinking of your audience.

Let's first play with the idea of questions for meetings.

I hope you would agree that questions are good for engagement. They pique our curiosity and get us thinking more, while demonstrating that the person asking the question is interested in our thoughts. One idea is to provide an agenda which asks questions instead of a list of topics. For example, 'What questions do you have, or information do you want to share?' instead of 'AOB'. If I received this on an agenda, my mind would start engaging with the question from the time I read it.

How can you include engaging questions in your talk? What questions will ignite the thinking of your audience? Remember to pause when you've asked them. Sometimes you might find it helpful at the start of a talk to let your audience know that you will be asking questions and allowing time, even a moment for reflecting. Most audiences know they're not supposed to answer aloud, but if you have any doubts you might want to suggest that they take note of their answer, tell the person next to them, or perhaps just answer in their own minds. If you are open to replies, make sure you've allowed time and that you can handle the interruption! If it's a long talk (more than 20 minutes), it can be very helpful to break it up with a question that allows people to participate with a show of hands, or even standing up. There's nothing quite like an opportunity to have a stretch if one has been sitting in an auditorium and the audience will generally appreciate it.

What questions can you include in your talk? Is there an 'if/then' question that might truly ignite the thinking of your audience? How can you apply this to interviews?

Place: *Producing a physical environment – the room, the listener, your body – that says, 'You matter'.*

Can you relate to the fact that we think, and therefore engage better, in a thoughtfully-prepared environment?[6] The need for safety and security is cited by Maslow as a basic need.[7] The component of Place considers that place is not just where we are physically or virtually, but also includes the body and clothes we inhabit.

Chapter 18

Where do you think best? What is present and what is absent? Can you recreate elements of this environment for your audience? Place is one good reason to dim lights in an auditorium and have bright lights on stage. It helps us to focus. In a training or learning space, I will always seek to reduce noise and visual distraction. Mind you, if you invite your audience to take notes, ensure the lighting facilitates this.

I have always found dress codes problematic and know from working at a school and having children of my own, that dress codes are a minefield. But what if we all dressed in a way that showed other people that they matter to us? People may not even register when you dress thoughtfully, but they will notice when what you wear jars with them. The process of thinking about this before we decide what to wear would be transformative, in our attitude as well as our clothing. It's also important for us to be comfortable if we are to pay attention to another; this includes both clothing and the chairs we occupy.

If we are standing, comfortable shoes that facilitate good posture matters. Heels tilt the body forward and can require locking our knees, which works against the voice. However, I also recognise that for many women, the height advantage and feeling of confidence that comes from heels can't be underestimated. Consider what works for you. In a training situation, this may mean balancing standing with sitting down, but remember that sitting down lowers the energy in the room, so time this carefully with the expected energy levels of your audience throughout the day.

When seated it's important that the chair allows you to place your bum in the back of the seat and your feet firmly on the ground to maximise your vocal strength, but also to create comfort and support. Are your trainees or audience seated comfortably where you are visible without them straining to see or hear?

The temperature of the room is a consideration, whether it's aircon, ventilation or fresh air. Also consider where people will store their coats and bags, with health and safety an additional consideration. A slide with this information can serve as a helpful prompt at the start of a training day. When you prepare the slide, it will act as a reminder to contact the venue if necessary. Fresh water should be made available for any meeting or event, for everyone. The proximity and location of toilet facilities is also important with regard to Place.

When Place says 'you matter' to the other person, you will consider all this in advance and prepare the room accordingly.

How will you use the consideration of Place to maximise the impact of your public speaking experience for your audience and yourself?

Chapter 19
What About Speaking without Slides, Props or Notes?

By now, you have hopefully begun to understand that *you* embody the message and bring it to your audience. If you are implementing the tools and techniques laid out so far, you should be well on your way to doing that effectively. You will embody the message by combining quality, well-structured content with attention, presence, vocal variety, gesture, and use of effective space. You may even use humour, which is excellent for engagement and receiving instant feedback from an audience. Of course, if the humour doesn't land, you will also receive instant feedback in the form of silence, so I suggest you reflect on your experience with humour before you make it a part of your strategy.

It is possible that slides, props and notes are not necessary to enhance your message. However, remembering what you learnt in chapter three about learning preferences, you may decide your talk would benefit from such enhancement. Once you have done what's necessary to embody the message with your whole self, the question you might ask is,

'What slides, props or notes could make the message more engaging?'

If the answer to the above question is none, you need to be confident that you can use your presence, your body and your voice to engage your audience and deliver your great content effectively for the duration of your talk.

If you feel props would make the message more engaging, then it's about carefully selecting the right ones to do so.

How can I best use notes?

Aide-mémoire is a lovely term for notes because it speaks of their purpose – they are a memory aid, a security blanket to help us stay on the right path and not lose our way.

What are your thoughts on using notes, or seeing others use them?

I have had the privilege of working with an experienced speaker, Frank,[1] who confessed that he struggled to speak without the use of notes. Is it a bad sign to use notes? We are accustomed to newsreaders and talk show hosts not using them, but they are using teleprompters. I've been reminded of that recently as I noticed an international host who has his own TV show very obviously reading from one. I wondered if his eyesight, like mine, has deteriorated during lockdown. Sadly, the result is that he comes across as less engaged with his television audience than when he refers to the notes in his hand. Anyone who watches TED or TEDx talks will be used to speakers who don't use notes, although I believe Alanna Shaikh gave the best talk on Coronavirus in March 2020, using notes. Presumably, the organisers wanted someone as quickly as possible; it's remarkable how little she referred to them.[2]

What are the benefits of speaking without notes? Firstly, you can make eye contact with your audience more of the time instead of referring to notes. Secondly, it can look more prepared or organised. Fear of judgement for using notes can be a reality, especially if we judge others for using them.

Why did my experienced client falter?

He had come up short during an after-dinner speech in which he was heckled. The comment was well received by both him and the audience; the only problem was it threw him, and he lost his train of thought. Having been impressed when the previous speaker didn't use notes, he decided to follow suit and left them at his table. Therein lay the problem and my first piece of advice.

1. Keep your notes to hand

How many times have you needed your car's airbag? If like me, your answer is never, I bet you still wouldn't go without one, even if the laws of the country allowed it. For many of us, using notes is not a sign of weakness; it's a sign of sanity!

It's respectful for a speaker to do their very best for the audience when they've been asked to speak. If you've put in the preparation and the practise, you will be able to relax and enjoy engaging your audience. However, if angst about losing your train of thought creates tension or fear, you will engage less effectively and the benefit of speaking without notes is lost.

Which leads me to my next point …

2. Be wise not weak

When I asked Frank why he felt he had to speak without notes, it emerged he thought using notes to be a sign of weakness and that his audience might expect it of him. If using notes means delivering a confident and coherent speech, it is wise, not weak. Don't be apologetic about it – the last thing your audience wants is for you to fail and notes can give you security and ensure you don't embarrass yourself or your audience as they cringe on your behalf! Having said that, over-dependence on notes is not good and there's no substitute for practise.

3. Be kind to yourself

We are our own worse critics! When I asked Frank if he would expect the same high standards of a fellow speaker, he admitted that he would not think less of another person for using notes. We need to be as kind to ourselves as we are to others.

4. Keep it neat

If you do decide to use notes, I recommend A5 or A6 card. Paper is flimsy and can easy fly off your lectern. If you don't have a lectern it will curl in your hands and not promote confidence. And finally, if you have more than one piece of paper, it will invariably be difficult to move from one sheet to the next. Anything larger will look awkward and A4 will not only make finding your place more challenging but could send a message to your audience that they're in for a long speech.

In 2021, the UK Prime Minister, undermined himself on an international scale at the COP26 Summit by losing his place in a sheaf of A4 paper and the results were excruciating. Although I can't imagine a valid excuse for him, there may be times when you don't have a choice and need to report from recently printed sheets that have been provided by someone else, or perhaps a report 'hot off the press'.

In this case, ensure they are printed one-sided, number them clearly, and always have a pen and at least one highlighter with you to highlight what you must not miss sharing. I like to use arrows and underline certain words too, but the main point is, personalise them, find a method that works for you to guide you through the notes. If it's a bound report, I recommend post-it notes. Strictly speaking, a report hot off the press or something provided by someone else are not notes, you're making notes from them to share with your audience. I would be inclined to contextualise this for my audience.

Once you've decided to have notes, they need to be very brief, perhaps the key word or idea that represents the main point, and/or the link to the next point. I don't recommend sentence starters or clever phrases you just don't want to forget. These tend to inhibit the flow of the speech and make you rigid about sticking to what you originally wrote, unless they are quotes you can't memorise, in which case people appreciate accuracy. Otherwise, trust that with the right amount of preparation and practise, you will remember what is salient. Realise that the audience don't know what you were planning to share and what they need to hear is engaging communication that flows easily between you.

5. Know your place

Having keywords or links on your notecards, you then need to practise, perhaps using my process below, using the cards and know where to find these prompts should you need to reference your notes. It's both effective and discreet to use your thumb along the side of your notes to ensure you keep your place when you make eye contact.

Often, I'm halfway or towards the end of a speech before I need to glance down to check what's next. I will still discreetly turn the cards as I progress. There's nothing worse than keeping the audience waiting while you figure out where to pick up the next point. If you've practised your speech with cards, you'll know exactly where you are. In the famous misogyny speech of Julia Gillard, former Australian Prime Minister, she demonstrates the mastery of using notes and re-finding one's place[3]. I highly recommend watching it for this reason.

6. Map it

We all have a favourite way of learning that is most effective for us. The spider diagram, see an example in Fig 7.1, with the topic in the middle and various legs leading us to the points in a speech may really work for some, while others have brains that work much better with a linear method which uses bullet points and perhaps arrows, as in Fig 7.2. These can be hand drawn and research has shown that our brain responds well to colour, if you would like to consider that.[4] Find out which works best for you, but if you can reduce your speech to either, you may be able to walk to the lectern with just one card. In fact, if you've practised enough with what's on the card, you may find that you don't even have to look at it, as you can see the next point or link in your mind's eye.

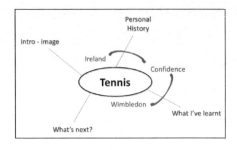 

Fig 7.1 and 7.2 - Some ideas for speech notes

7. Take a journey

I had intended sharing some wise words with Frank about having links between his ideas so that he could easily remember the next point, as it flowed naturally from the one before. However, this very experienced speaker had already done this, and in one section, the links were based on an imagined walk from one place to the next through the city on which his speech was based. But it emerged he wasn't using this as a memory tool! When he consciously realised he had very strong links between his ideas, and wrote these down, he had no problem remembering what came next. If you create a speech or presentation that flows naturally from one idea to the other, it will make the speech more fluent to deliver and to hear.

Although it won't always suit a speech to imagine walking from one place to the next, you can do this using a very clever trick when practising. Either walk through your house and deliver each part in a different room so that on the night, you can mentally go on that journey and remember what you said in each room, or, if you know your venue, you can 'place' each idea in a different part of the room. For example, your introduction is the door at the back, your first idea the window on the right, then the window on the left, the next the light fitting in the middle, and so on. Of course, it's important to make eye contact with your audience in between!

8. Consider not writing your speech down

Having delivered eight out of ten speeches in my Competent Toastmasters[5] journey, a well-meaning fellow speaker said, 'You really need to lose your notes.' I thought about it carefully, and then proceeded to complete the journey reliant on notes. When I moved to the UK, I turned a new leaf. I realised that my problem was not my over-dependence on notes but my attachment to my clever turn of phrase in the speech I had written. The only way to break out of this habit was to not write my speech down in the first place. You see, I realised that if the speech came out of my head and landed on paper, I struggled to bring it back to life and out through my mouth. But if I didn't commit it to paper, it could only come from my head and my heart!

Since then, I rarely stand up with more than a few points on a card. Therefore, I share ideas and not paragraphs. This is the only way I have succeeded in losing notes and might be worth considering if you also struggle in this area.

As a coach, I believe that every presentation problem can be overcome through listening, reflection, reworking and rehearsing. I listen and share some ideas; the learner reflects and reworks their delivery and through rehearsal, they can usually remove the obstacle to good speaking, or improve their presentation. The same applies to the use of notes.

In the case of Frank, a session to focus on speaking without notes turned into a session about using notes effectively, minimising the use of notes and perhaps not needing to use those that you have. The bottom line is that you have choices. Make the right ones that work for you in every given situation.

A note on working the room, including eye contact

In Chapter Four, I made suggestions about where to place your gaze to maximise confidence and connection. This does not change if you use slides, props and notes.

Chapter 19

Eye contact engages your audience, it says, 'I see you' and 'this is for you'. People who don't make eye contact are in danger of losing their audience, although I have worked with clients and dinner party guests whose autism has meant that eye contact is superfluous as they don't like or make it as an audience member. However, it's safe to assume that a room will consist of a variety of neurotypical and neurodiverse people and I would therefore encourage the use of eye contact. Combined with the use of your home point, it should be a gaze for a moment, a second or two, before moving around the audience in a reasonable facsimile of an M, W, or ∞. Any shorter has the danger of being a meaningless glance, any longer can feel like a stare.

Case study: Rhys

If you are a particularly nervous public speaker, which will hopefully reduce as you engage with this book, it can be nerve wracking to make eye contact with people in the room. This was the case with Rhys, who had grown up with a controlling, critical parent.

We were working on his elevator pitch as he ran his own business, and networking was an important means of marketing. But how could people put their confidence in his excellent ability in his business if he came across as underconfident when he spoke about it? Having worked on content and delivery, he was still struggling when he tried to make eye contact with fellow attendees.

I asked him to name a few friendly faces in the room, people who he found friendly to speak to in one-to-one conversation. He was immediately able to name at least three. I suggested he add these two or three people as home points, depending on where they were sitting, until he felt confident enough to include others.

It worked. After the first time he implemented this, he went on to add less friendly-looking faces in the room as his confidence grew.

Note: As an audience member, please do your best to engage with a speaker. Looking at your phone or elsewhere can make their turn to speak more of a challenge. Even better, smile! You will make such a difference to them, and it will undoubtedly gain you a business advantage.

Chapter 20

How Can I Best Use Slides and Other Visual Aids?

Basic principles

There are books, videos and trainers who specialise in slide presentation skills and who keep up with the latest developments and trends. Were I to capture them here, they would be potentially out of date by the time you're reading it. In my work, slides are a visual aid and are an extension of the main work of embodying the message. Therefore, it is my intention to set out some basic principles to ensure you enhance what you are already doing well to embody the message. Once you're thinking along the right lines with the basics in place for you and your audience, you can take your own journey to add the level of sophistication to your slides and visual aids that are right for you.

Principle One: Less is more

You've heard this principle through the book, and it applies equally to visual aids. How simple can you keep it? KISS – Keep It Super Simple! Recently, I saw an online TEDx speaker use a beach ball as a visual aid to illustrate how we supress our emotions, 'like holding a beach ball constantly under water'.[1] She didn't use water, asking us instead to imagine it, but her words and movements aptly illustrated how emotions are pushed down in this way, until they eventually can't be supressed any longer. She was able to place the ball to one side and reach for it again at the end to remind us of her point. Her visual aid powerfully reinforced it.

The same goes for slides. How few do you need to enhance your message? This is why the processes outlined in Chapter 15 suggest creating your presentation outline without a slide deck first. They are simply visual aids to add emphasis or illustrate a point in a way that is more impactful for your audience. But in the same way that over-emphasis in modulation is no emphasis at all, too many slides will fail to highlight your message if you use them for everything.

Principle Two: Don't look back!

If you use slides, it's vital that you remain engaged with your audience. It's a common error to look at the slides behind you. Ideally, you should either know your presentation so well that you know exactly when to cue the next slide, or you have a laptop in view that shows you what's on the screen. PowerPoint's presenter mode can show a view with the next slide and notes visible too. Gesturing to information on the slide without looking should be adequate from time to time. There is an Indian text on dance which states, 'where the hands go the eyes follow'[2] and this is equally true for public speaking. Ideally, look at your audience while you gesture to the screen.

Principle Three: Use optimal position

When using visual aids, position them as much as possible where you can still make eye contact with your audience. It's vital that your audience can see them clearly, in terms of both size and position.

Don't get lit up or partially lit up by the screen! It might be worth packing masking tape in your kit to mark where your optimal position range is on a stage. TED have their famous red dot for the cameras, but it's also helpful for this reason.

The next five principles are based on using PowerPoint or similar slide presentation tools as a visual aid. My experience in this field is reinforced by the findings of David J.P. Phillips, whose work is based on neuroscience and biology, who urges us to "cognitively and psychologically optimise [our] PowerPoints".[3]

Principle Four: Work with working memory

Studies have repeatedly shown that we don't have good working memories[4] unless we're helped to remember using various methods including reinforcement, repetition and revision. Being bombarded with too much information on a slide will not accomplish this. Phillips states that we forget 90% of what we hear within 30 seconds. The remaining principles will suggest how to help your audience remember better.

Principle Five: Use one message per slide

Multi-tasking effectively is a myth; we just do two or more things badly. With this in mind, what one message do you want to get across in your slide? The brain will only engage effectively with one so don't expect your audience to choose. That message needs to reinforce what you're saying, or the audience will be conflicted. Therefore, decide what one message to select for each slide.

When the audience don't need to look at the screen, use the blank screen feature on your clicker or 'B' on your keyboard to blank it and bring the focus back to you. In PowerPoint, you can also set your presentation as your virtual background for online presentations. You can then build in blank or neutral slides and drag the image of yourself to dominate the screen, reducing it again as you return to a message slide. This requires practise and an easeful communication around it to your audience. Because you may be using different software, I recommend you use the Help feature to identify the functions available.

Principle Six: Don't pit listening against reading

The language centre of the brain reads and listens to process information. If we are listening to the speakers' words, we cannot read other words, and vice versa. At best, we switch intermittently from one to the other. The result is that our audience cannot listen or read properly, and the message is lost.

The solution is to use contrast to highlight a headline word or phrase that you're speaking, to reinforce your point and then use 'Animations' with the dim feature to highlight the next word or phrase you're speaking. Your audience's eyes will follow the point you are making, and they will listen to what you are saying with that visual anchor.

Principle Seven: Use dark backgrounds and light text

Remember, *you* are the presentation. If your slides are on a light background, you dim in significance if the projector is on a big screen. Even if you're using a smaller screen in a meeting room, people with dyslexia (approximately one in six people or 15% of the population[5]) struggle with reading dark words on a white background. It's also easier on the eyes and counters screen fatigue, particularly in an online setting.

You need to be the most contrast-rich object. This may mean finding images with transparent backgrounds and having a logo which will contrast with your background. See Fig 8 where my logo, usually black, is white and semi-transparent so as to not compete with the message.

Fig. 8. Slide for showing the advantage of one message. The question at the top is from the previous slide.

Principle Eight: Size matters

The default on PowerPoint suggests large headings and smaller points. But the heading is not usually what we want people to remember. The important message in your slide should also be the biggest. Fig 8 above illustrates this too.

Use Slide Master to change the size of your headline versus body text. You will not need to bother with different sizes for different levels as you won't need bullets or have different sizes; you are using animation and the dim feature instead.

Principle Nine: Limit objects to six

You will have picked up by now that the primary goal of presenting is to engage the audience with as little work from them as possible. Counting takes up to 500% more energy than seeing, so provide something your audience can see, not what they have to process. Ideally, you want your audience to see your slides and engage with your message, not expend energy processing your slide content.

Our brain can see five objects at a glance, according to Phillips; six facilitates engagement without overwhelm. Any more than that takes exponentially longer to process.

You have probably realised by now that applying these principles will potentially mean creating more slides. The quantity of slides is not an issue for your audience; rather, it's the quantity of information per slide.

When considering what to select for a slide, remember that we have limits to our perception. Our eyes focus on four things: moving objects, signalling colours (red, orange and yellow), contrast-rich objects and big objects. How will you use this information to make engaging with your audience an enjoyable and memorable experience?

Case study: Peter

"Really, really impressed with how you've transformed your speaking opportunity into an inspirational speech that you're really enjoying now. I'm just struck by the fact that both it and you were competent to begin with, but in retrospect it was rather dull, and you wanted to *be* more and your audience to *receive* more. It's definitely 'there' now … I honestly think it's going to be fun and when it's over you're going to be so chuffed with what you've achieved."

Chapter 20

This is what I wrote to Peter towards the end of our work together. He runs the European division of an international company and was asked to present at their annual conference in the US. Conscious of the high energy presentations of the American speakers, he wanted to ensure he engaged his audience and that they enjoyed what he had to share.

Peter is an expert in his field and can speak about it fluently to his team and his distributors. Being a modest Englishman who does not seek the limelight, he was prepared to do his part in speaking and wanted to do his division proud, while still retaining his authenticity. Alongside the foundation work outlined in Section Two, we looked at the ideas he had for his presentation. Once he had identified what he wanted his audience to think, feel and do as a result of his talk, he started thinking about what content would accomplish that result. Once that was ready, he went away to put together a slide outline that supported his words.

He returned with the skeleton in place - what he *had* to share. We were now ready to add the meat and flesh!

Fuelled by the engagement he was now experiencing with his audience in mind, the ideas began to flow. The accomplishment of targets, increase in market share and other good news were now brought alive with ideas of how to demonstrate this in an exciting way. A short video of influencers and two other images of notable product users were incorporated into the presentation to bring the data to life. Slide animation ensured that the audience weren't conflicted about reading or listening. All the principles above were adhered to as the slide deck came together.

There was no information overload and Peter was front and centre stage with his slides supporting him. He was enjoying the prospect of speaking which infused his voice with energy and led to him smiling, something which had been a struggle up to this point. As we reached the end of our time together, the best word I could use to describe Peter was 'transformed'. He had even become playful about the presentation, adding some iconic film music to his entrance slide. He knew that the audience would love the connection with Oxford, home of his company division. It provided a highly impactful start to his talk, on par with his fellow-speakers, while retaining the authenticity of Peter's style.

This transformation happens when audience, speaker and visual aids come together in perfect balance.

How can I best use other visual aids?

Principle Three above, mentions the importance of visibility and eye-contact when it comes to using visual aids. Visibility also means that they need to be the right size for all of your audience to see and the colour must contrast with what you're wearing and your background. A speaker should not have to call out, 'Can you see this at the back?' It's your responsibility to plan so that you know everyone can see and is an important reason for a recce of the room in advance, if possible. If you wish to ensure visibility, an invitation to anyone who is struggling to see to move forward or come sit at the front is different, and an inclusive invitation for those visually impaired or struggling because of a height disadvantage or being wheelchair bound.

It is also imperative to ensure that your visual aids are practical and possible to transport, as well as protected from breakage or spillage.

Case study: Madhav and Callum (see Fig. 9)

A favourite speech I saw years ago, focused on priorities. The speaker, Madhav, used two large glass containers with sand, pebbles and rocks to fill them with during the course of the talk. I've never forgotten the message as Madhav filled the jars first one way and then another, demonstrating that if we start with our biggest priorities first, the smaller and then the smallest fit in our days or lives. The reality of seeing both before our eyes was powerful. In the last two years, I've seen that speech done again, with the same theme. This time, the speaker, Callum, used slides to demonstrate. It was also impactful, but

I imagine less so to anyone who hadn't been treated to the live demonstration I witnessed. I don't imagine the impact difference was significant and the message was engaging in both instances. Decide for yourself in context of all the other decisions you have to make.

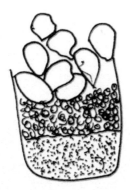 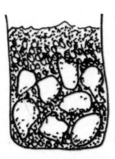

Fig. 9 Case Study illustrating the rock, pebbles and sand analogy

Visual aids that can be shared with or used by the audience can also be impactful. If we can appeal to all five senses to connect with an audience, this is a means of utilising touch. Going back to my writing on VARK in Section One, you are also offering a kinaesthetic experience when audience participation is involved. It's especially important in a training presentation. It's worth noting that with COVID-19 still present in the world as I write this book and new variants on the horizon, the choice to involve people in touching the same object or objects can be more complex than before. It's possible that passing something around a room can be a distraction. Depending on numbers, you need to ensure everyone has an equal opportunity to experience it before your talk ends, or that you have multiples of the item. Simply think it through and make a considered judgement. I've had good engagement and interaction with a talk where different visual aids have been placed on each table that referenced a point in my talk. The audience have enormous fun showing the prop to everyone and anticipating when their object would be spoken about – and these were mostly older businessmen! I believe in having as much fun as possible with my talks and laughter is a great stimulant, but I do build in time for the responses and reactions.

If you run your own business, consider using a branded visual aid to give your audience to use while you're talking and perhaps to keep. It will not only remind them of your talk but connect it to you and your company. A branded golf ball during a presentation on human movement is one that a client of mine has used to great effect. A stress ball from a mindfulness coach is another. Consider whether your visual aid or aids are most suited to provide before or share during a presentation. It may be that you simply decide to provide one afterwards and engage your audience otherwise when you are speaking.

Flip charts are still a popular visual aid and learning tool. They are a wonderful way to brainstorm and gather ideas. It's also a good place to park an idea or question you're not ready to answer yet. It's vital that what you write or draw is visible to your audience and is legible. Practise if this is new to you and also consider prepopulating the flip chat before you begin, at least in part. Ensure there are enough pages, that you have packed your markers and they are all working, every time. Do not trust the venue to do this. Pack Blue Tac or similar if you want to tear out and display a page, but ensure you have the venue's permission to do so on their surfaces.

I'm not a fan of handouts for a few reasons mentioned elsewhere, but if this is your visual aid of choice, consider it not being a visual aid during the presentation, but something you email before or afterwards. This will be better for the environment and only those who value them will print them out. If you offer to provide them afterwards, it's also a means of gathering data on your attendees, if that is something you value.

Interactive Whiteboards have increased in popular usage in recent years and can provide a powerful interactive experience, especially online. *'Scribble on your slides; it makes them so much more interesting'* is the advice of creative collaboration expert, Penny Pullen. It's basically combining a slide presentation with an electronic flipchart. There are two tips I will include here; buy a decent graphics tablet and practise using it until you're doing it competently before an audience.

Do I need an equipment checklist?

In drama circles, the word 'prop' is used to describe a portable object used on the set of a play or film. It's an abbreviation of the word property and doesn't include furniture or costumes. Every stage manager will have a Props List and the props in place before the play or scene opens and they will be returned at the end, or at least before the scene begins again. It is worth having a similar list for every public speaking opportunity you have, and even more worthwhile using it!

I have a checklist for each type of speaking engagement I do, from training to keynote speaking, to wedding fairs. And because I customise each message for my audience, each checklist will change accordingly, with some standard items. It is best that you do the same for your situation. There are some examples on the internet, but your Props List is likely to be as unique as your talk will be.

Chapter 21
What Might Helpful Feedback Look Like for a Speaker?

I love feedback. This is because we can't be both the speaker and the audience, so we depend on others to help us understand what we're doing well, and what we can do better. It's only recently that I realised people have a lot of negative connotations around it. However, if one knows how to request and give feedback appropriately, it's incredibly helpful and almost always free. So, embrace it. People love to help but don't always know how.

A selection of feedback tools

Let me share my favourite feedback tools with you and you can decide how to mix and match them, depending on what you find helpful. But I would urge you to give people specific criteria. Otherwise, you might find what they say unhelpful, too much, or even hurtful. I recently heard someone compare feedback to a gift: we don't always like what we're given, and we have the power to choose what to keep.

Here are the three tools I use most often:

- The three Ss
- Retrospective questions
- The BOOST model of feedback

The three Ss

In my Time to Think training we learnt that appreciation needs to be sincere, specific and succinct. The same can be said for feedback. We need to mean it sincerely and kindly, we need to avoid being vague and should take the trouble to note specific examples when we reference anything the person has said or done. And we need to keep it brief. The last is particularly true of negative feedback. I find myself couching negative feedback in other comments so that they land more gently. It takes twice as long. But if I have the courage to 'say it (kindly) like it is', the recipient appreciates it more and can handle it in an environment where there is social permission.

Ask and give others permission to be sincere, specific and succinct when you request feedback.

Retrospective questions[1]

I have Jason Lane, founder and CEO of Innovista Oxford to thank for introducing these to me. He spoke about it in the context of leaders getting feedback from their staff to close the blind spot in the Johari Window[2] – what I don't know about myself that others know.

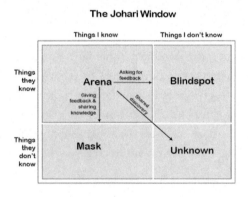

Fig. 10: The Arena will expand and the blind spot will reduce if you ask for feedback

I've adapted this for public speaking feedback as follows:

How did I experience it?
What went well?
What could I do better next time?

You then supply this to the event organiser, your liaison person at the event, or a trusted member of the audience if you have such a person attending. For your own reflective feedback, you might insert an additional question, 'What have I learned?'

The BOOST model of feedback

If you have an opportunity to practise feedback, you might wish to use or request the BOOST model of feedback[3] as a measuring rod:

B – Is it balanced? We hear better when we are in an environment of encouragement. All negative or all positive feedback isn't going to help us. Feedback has got a very bad rap because too many people believe it to be about faults and failings. Focus on how you experienced it, what was good and what could be better, in a ratio of at least 2:1, ideally 5:1.

O – Is it objective? This is where asking someone who knows us too well can be tricky. You need to give or receive feedback for the situation and audience you are addressing. Getting personal is not helpful. Find a way to share something that could be said to anyone doing or saying that specific thing by another person, besides you.

O – Is it observed? Base feedback on what you are seeing and hearing now and ensure that it's evidence based.

S – Is it specific? Vague comments are challenging to address. Be specific about what you heard or saw and what the impact was.

T – Is it timely? Give or ask for feedback at the first available opportunity. The learning window from a particular experience closes as time moves on and new challenges come our way. Keep it relevant.

If you do have someone kind enough to give you feedback using the criteria you request, the best response is 'thank you' and nothing else. It's tempting to explain or justify, but if it's after the event, it's not relevant and can prevent that person from wanting to give feedback again. As the saying goes, 'don't shoot the messenger'!

A word about unsolicited feedback

While positive feedback on your speech is wonderful, the main issue with feedback of the constructive kind is that many people who give it don't necessarily know how to help you with what you're not getting right, much as an audience member would be unable to direct a professional actor. This is one good reason to proceed with caution when giving or receiving feedback. I make it a policy to never tell someone what they're doing wrong unless I have the time and ability to give them a proven solution.

Most importantly: don't give unsolicited feedback. If someone is polite enough to listen or agree when you offer feedback, they are unlikely to appreciate you for your time and wisdom, unless you are exclusively complimentary. And you really should be charging if you're professionally qualified to give 'constructive criticism'.

Prepare yourself in advance for people who may approach with well-meaning advice or feedback. If you have any level of anxiety about public speaking, you are more vulnerable to being offended right after you've spoken. Here are a few ideas.

- Go ahead and listen but be prepared for anything!
- If they launch into feedback without asking permission, stop them politely, using a 'stop' hand-gesture if they're a bit thick-skinned and carry on. Thank them and let them know you've already got a trusted 'other' supplying feedback with specific criteria. Smile and tell them how much you appreciated the offer, though.
- If they offer feedback, ask them how much they charge for it. If the answer is that they don't, you could ask what criteria they

are measuring it against, 'just to ensure we're on the same page'. This should at least help them to think about what you need to hear, rather than them sharing their expertise, as is often the case.

- Let them know that you need some fresh air or to use the facilities or catch up with someone before they leave. Smile and tell them how much you appreciated the offer, though.

As a member of the Professional Speaking Association of UK and Ireland, we have a 'Showcase' slot in the programme where speakers get to practise some of their material and receive feedback. The host will always let the room know the acceptable channels for this and is quite clear in letting people know that unsolicited feedback is not welcome. Hopefully, by now you will realise that you don't have to welcome it either.

A celebrity case study: Coaching Sherlock

In 2010, the BBC released a drama where actor Benedict Cumberbatch played Sherlock Holmes. In a later episode, Sherlock's Best Man speech at Dr Watson's wedding epitomised all that is good, bad and ugly in public speaking.

As people don't always understand what's involved in voice and speech coaching, I wrote a showcase to demonstrate how I might coach anyone with their upcoming speech, presentation or reading, wedding or otherwise, by providing professional feedback.

For the purposes of demonstrating this, I imagined taking Sherlock through his speech as if it were a practise, knowing I could anticipate the reactions of the audience.

To begin with, I would explain that public speaking, whether it's a pitch, presentation, interview or occasional speech has two elements as you can see in Fig 11.

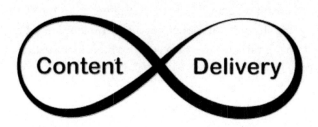

Fig 11

Many people can focus on one at the expense of the other, but they are equally important. We struggle to engage with a monotonous or 'shouty' voice, even if the content is wonderful. However, stunning delivery of poor content is what we commonly refer to as bullshit.

If you haven't heard, or can't remember it, the speech transcript[4] is below. Watching the video will be essential to understanding the feedback on delivery, however, and this is available on BBC iPlayer.[5]

SHERLOCK: Done that. ... Done that ... Done that bit ... Done that bit ... Done that bit ... Hmm ... *(turns to John)*

I'm afraid, John, I can't congratulate you. *(Looking at the guests)* All emotions, and in particular love, stand opposed to the pure, cold reason I hold above all things. A wedding is, in my considered opinion, nothing short of a celebration of all that is false and specious and irrational and sentimental in this ailing and morally compromised world. *(The guests begin to look uncomfortable)*

Today we honour the death-watch beetle that is the doom of our society and, in time – one feels certain – our entire species. *(The guests stare at him.)*

But anyway ... let's talk about John.

JOHN (quietly): Please.

SHERLOCK (looking up again): If I burden myself with a little help-mate during my adventures, it is not out of sentiment or caprice – it is that he has many fine qualities of his own that he has overlooked in his obsession with me. *(Greg laughs silently.)*

Indeed, any reputation I have for mental acuity and sharpness comes, in truth, from the extraordinary contrast John so selflessly provides. *(John sighs heavily, while Mary frowns.)*

It is a fact, I believe, that brides tend to favour exceptionally plain bridesmaids for their big day. There is a certain analogy there, I feel. *(Janine stares up at him and the other two bridesmaids look uncomfortable.)* ... and contrast is, after all, God's own plan to enhance the beauty of his creation ... *(The vicar smiles.)* Or it would be if God were not a ludicrous fantasy designed to provide a career opportunity for the family idiot. *(Mary face-palms and John is half-hiding behind his clasped hands. The vicar looks at Sherlock grimly.)*

The point I'm trying to make is that I am the most unpleasant, rude, ignorant and all-round obnoxious arsehole that anyone could possibly have the misfortune to meet. *(He looks at the vicar.)* I am dismissive of the virtuous ... *(He turns to Janine.)* ... unaware of the beautiful ... *(He turns towards Mary and John.)* ... and uncomprehending in the face of the happy. So, if I didn't understand I was being asked to be best man, it is because I never expected to be anybody's best friend. Certainly not the best friend of the bravest and kindest and wisest human being I have ever had the good fortune of knowing. *(Mary smiles proudly at her husband.)*

John, I am a ridiculous man ... *(John smiles and nods his agreement.)* redeemed only by the warmth and constancy of your friendship. But, as I'm apparently your best friend, I cannot congratulate you on your choice of companion. *(He looks down then smiles slightly.)* Actually, now I can. *(The guests murmur. John and Mary smile.)*

Mary, when I say you deserve this man, it is the highest compliment of which I am capable. John, you have endured war, and injury, and tragic loss ... so sorry again about that last one ... *(he straightens up again)* ... so know this: today you sit between the woman you have made your wife and the man you have saved – in short, the two people who love you most in all this world. And I know I speak for Mary as well when I say we will never let you down, and we have a lifetime ahead to prove that. *(Mrs Hudson whimpers John turns to Mary and whispers)*

JOHN: If I try and hug him, stop me.

MARY: Certainly not *(She pats his arm).*

SHERLOCK: Ah, yes. Now on to some funny stories about John ... *(he looks seeing the guests crying. Quick fire)* What's wrong? What happened? Why are you all doing that? John? *(Molly smiles proudly at him.).*

MRS HUDSON (tearfully): Oh, Sherlock! *(Sherlock looks down at John.)*

SHERLOCK: Did I do it wrong?

JOHN *(standing up):* No, you didn't. Come here. *(He pulls him into a tight hug. The guests break into applause).*

SHERLOCK: I haven't finished yet.

JOHN: Yeah, I know, I know.

SHERLOCK (talking over the applause): So, on to some funny stories ...

JOHN: Can you – can you wait 'til I sit down?

Notwithstanding, this speech provides an excellent exposition of Sherlock's character, consistent with every other episode, and that the first part makes the end all the more meaningful, my professional feedback regarding Sherlock's speech would be as follows. You may find it helpful to pass this on to the person providing you with feedback to give them some idea of the aspects they can encourage and assist you with. I've highlighted the aspects for this reason.

Appearance is important and Sherlock is well presented with good posture. **Posture** is not only important for appearance but vital for vocal strength and projection. However, he does compromise this posture later when he bends over to shuffle through his notes. In doing so, he disengages from his audience and presents as disorganised. I would advise him on the effective use of notes.

Sherlock's **vocal quality** is strong. He is projecting and using appropriate **volume**. There is also very good use of **pause** as he greets everyone. Then he lets himself down when he adds a group of people he doesn't know how to describe and descends into 'ums'. **Practise** would eliminate this as he would commit to his choice of words. Clearing his throat and muttering to himself in front of everyone is not ideal; I would share a few recommendations to counter these easily avoidable issues.

I like his **use of humour** regarding the telegrams, but this does spill over into sarcasm and genuine disregard for the feelings of others. Rattling off the telegrams revealed his disinterest; this will not engage an audience. There are several occasions where he could benefit from some guidance on the content of his speech to avoid the audience's evident discomfort, as Sherlock demonstrates his intellectual superiority, but also his inability to share the truth wisely. People can struggle in knowing the difference between wit and giving offence. It's got more to do with sensitivity than common sense, something Sherlock the sociopath clearly lacks!

Benedict Cumberbatch is a master of **pace** in all his roles, but this speech exemplifies it beautifully. His ability to vary his pace from almost high speed to funereal is highly effective in engaging his audience and appropriately matches the content of his speech. Without wonderful articulation and clarity, few people can master this contrast effectively. As gifted an actor as he is, he wasn't born with this ability and has invested years of learning and practise in his speaking craft. Exercises on **articulation** and learning how to vary pace are a vital part of any speech coaching. It's clear that he has had coaching[6].

Have you noticed the one homage to a **smile** during Sherlock's speech? Smiling naturally not only helps a speaker make a connection with their audience but is far more genial in both appearance and **tone**. It will even help a speaker get away with some of the inappropriate remarks they may wish to make!

The next part of the speech is a wonderful recovery as he speaks sincerely about friendship. **Sincerity** in public speaking is vital;

breathing and relaxation exercises aid a speaker to connect with the emotional centre so that the spoken word is true. It's clear that he's touched the hearts of his audience by their reaction and the day is almost saved. But he does focus on drawing attention to himself too much. No effective speaker does this. There is no reason for fear or nerves in a speech – it's not about you; it's about your message and the audience; you are simply the privileged messenger!

If this wedding were for real, we could bin the first half of Sherlock's speech during sessions. What we're now left with, except for the mumbling and shuffling of notes, is the potential for a fine and true Best Man's speech. It would be better to have a three-minute sincere, well-delivered speech than subjecting an audience to ten minutes of discomfort - and knowing when to end it, which Sherlock clearly doesn't!

Those who deliver readings or wedding speeches are chosen, not because of their ability, but because of their importance to the bride and groom. For this reason, there is a liberal amount of compassion available. However, it's a kindness not to stretch this goodwill too far.[7]

A word about wedding feedback

Feedback can be a challenge for those who have wedding speeches to deliver. You might want the contents to remain a surprise for all the guests. Therefore, many of the obvious people you might ask are attending and it could be awkward to ask someone who's not on the list. Is there someone you work with you can ask? Or a good neighbour, obviously not one expecting an invitation!

I've enjoyed coaching grooms, best men, fathers of the brides and readers. It's probably the most fun part of my work. If you're not in a position to invest in a coach, ensure the person you ask can be trusted to give fair, honest and objective feedback. This maxim applies no matter what the occasion.

Finally, do remember to act on the feedback you are given if you believe it could help the audience's experience, it can be a game-changer.

Chapter 22
Effective Communication for Interviews – What's Special?

Success for a job interview, even if you don't get the job

In this final chapter, I've chosen to focus on interview situations. When it comes to effective spoken communication, job interviews are one of the greatest opportunities to shine. Obviously, there is a lot more involved, often long before you have an opportunity to speak. For this reason, I will share my knowledge and experience on the parts that relate to speaking.

It's important to identify your success criteria for a job interview beyond getting the job. This applies for a proposal submission, a gig and a sales pitch too, anywhere that you're essentially selling yourself and your skills to a panel or audience. I will refer to all of them as interviews for the sake of simplicity. The truth is that there are some interviews where there is going to be a better candidate or a better product. There are also situations where the person or product has already been decided but the process must take place to meet some externally required criteria. An example would be where an internal applicant is favoured for a job, but the company has to advertise more widely. This is why it's not as simple as 'getting the job/gig/pitch' – you will feel defeated if that's your only criteria.

So how will you know if you've given it your best shot?

Because the job market changes frequently and is so diverse across roles and countries, it's not the remit of this book to give advice in the career coaching space. The preparation requirements are bespoke for each candidate at a given time. My speciality is preparing candidates for showing up with confidence for their interview. However, here are a couple of ideas I believe will help any interview candidates prior to this.

Consider setting up an Informational Interview. As networking is the primary way people are getting jobs in the 2020s, building strategic relationships with contacts at the companies you prefer is a great strategy.

Have an elevator pitch for networking on and offline. In the context of job hunting, this is two minutes in which you can share who you are, what your qualifications and/or experience is and what work you'd love to do. Whilst ideally, that is part of a conversation in which you're asked for that information during a two-way conversation, it helps to have all this information ready in a succinct format so that you can share it with confidence and are able to customise it for the person or group you are addressing. It needs to be fluid, interesting and relevant. See Appendix 2 for an outline to create an Elevator Pitch.

If you are called for Interview:

1. Celebrate! It's important to pause and celebrate your accomplishments at every stage. Interviewing can be a lengthy and arduous process.
2. Research the organisation, the job and the team.
3. Find out as much as you can about the interviewers, the interview location, and the area.
4. Practise answering the questions you may be asked.
5. Understand how to be fully present on camera, on the telephone and in person so that you maximise audience engagement. Dress using the component of Place as your criteria, as outlined in Chapter 18.
6. Complete the Rondo Sequence on the day of each interview and interview stage, as close as is practically possible to the

interview. Practise breathing and maintain good breath control throughout.

7. Be ready in good time and without distractions. That means switching off notifications on your phone, switching off your phone, and being on site 15 minutes early if the interview is in person.

8. In the interview, if you are offered a drink, consider choosing water, unless hot beverages are being made for or by all. Apart from the general reasons given elsewhere, it avoids the conversation about how you like your beverages and is less problematic with potential accidents. It also creates the least fuss for your potential employer whilst accepting their hospitality.

9. Always remember your Bespoken Technique of Posture and the other techniques of effective communication, especially smiling and pause.

10. Know how to communicate the value you can bring to the organisation as succinctly as possible. Know how to articulate a negative experience or weakness without shame, fear or embarrassment. Have judicious responses for gaps on your CV. Your words, body language and tone of voice need to be congruent and confident in both positive and negative communication.

11. Think about where you might wish to be in five years' time in that role. It's a very popular question and if they don't ask it, you might wish to ask them when it's your turn to ask questions.

12. Read body language throughout for signs that you need to finish up or that they may wish you to expand.

13. Know your rights and how to respectfully handle any questions that might be inappropriate.

14. Remember to thank everyone for their time and the opportunity to interview. If you are very keen for this job, a hand-written 'thank you' note in the post is always delightful to receive.

15. If you are unsuccessful at any stage, remember to ask for feedback so that you can improve areas for your next application. Never defend yourself or argue; just say 'thank you'. If you are successful, celebrate!
16. If you are struggling with several aspects of this process, consider reaching out to a coach who can be alongside you in the process. It's a worthwhile investment as the return on investment can be ten or twenty-fold.

Questions, questions, questions!

Getting into a good rhythm of answering questions well is vital as you approach interview dates.

Motivational and behavioural or competency-type questions will require much practise as this is not something we generally do every day. Motivational questions ask you why-type questions, behavioural /competency are about how you would do or behave in certain situations.

Have three to five good questions ready to ask the panel. Multiple questions are important because they may answer some of your questions during the interview. One of my favourite questions, that is rarely addressed in an interview is, "What do you most like about working here?" Apart from providing good information, it shows a genuine interest in the people you may work with in the future and most people enjoy others taking an interest in them.

I would avoid questions about salary, leave and promotion in the first interview. Asking about timeframes for decision-making regarding the role is always good to end with too, unless you have been provided with this information in advance. Avoid asking questions you're supposed to know the answers to; it will show that you haven't prepared adequately and potentially irritate your interviewers. They often provide this information, so they don't have to answer it multiple times!

Competency questions and the STAR framework

Competency-based questions are often used by employers to ascertain if candidates possess the qualities or skills that are required for the role. These should be easy to find in the job and person specification. Here are a few examples:

- Tell us about an occasion when you have had to manage your time around a deadline. What happened and what did you have to do?
- Can you give an example of working as part of a team to complete a project or task? What role did you play and what was the outcome?
- Describe a time when you have had to deal with someone who was angry or upset. How did you deal with it?

The interviewer is using these questions to establish if you have the skills and qualities they need for the role. While it is important to sound natural in your answers, it's helpful to have practised responses using a frame that outlines the example you use, whilst giving evidence that you have what's needed.

STAR is an effective framework to use and is an acronym for Situation, Task, Action, Result. This is how it works, and the complete answers should take about two minutes to deliver. You can always include more detail.

- Situation – What was the context? This is a brief, broad description of what was happening and what was required.
- Task – What was the objective or purpose? Zone in on the task or tasks that was required of you.
- Action – How did you approach the task and what did you do? This is an opportunity to share your skills.
- Result – What was the outcome? It's important to provide a three-fold result. What was the result for you personally, for the team and for the organisation? Your personal takeaway

could be from something you learnt, to a promotion; both are equally valuable.

Attempt to give a balanced response. In my experience, candidates can spend too much time setting up the situation or task and forget to give the result or just give a one-line answer.

As requests for interviews come in, it's a good idea to create some sample questions for the role, enlisting a friend or partner to brainstorm with you. Don't write down complete answers, practise orally or just make note of the key points against the letters STAR. This will help you to recall what you need should a similar question be asked. Ensure you're listening carefully to the questions asked and answer as naturally and thoughtfully as possible. Over-practised responses come across poorly in interview and can lead to interviewers asking progressively more difficult questions until they get to one that is answered *ex tempore*. Having listened carefully, remember to pause and think before responding. Far from coming across badly, it should communicate your regard for the question and person asking it.

Case study – Interview technique

Before lockdowns normalised online coaching in 2020, I had the privilege of coaching a client in South Africa on Skype. He was struggling to find work, and his mother, Beverley Arnold, put us in touch. She knew about my work from a conversation in South Africa in 2018.

Tyrone presented as an authentic, personable young man. However, I could see that in an interview he would come across as casual, laid back and potentially too familiar. It was important for me that he retained his authenticity while understanding that a future employer needed to see a candidate who was competent, confident and would take the requirements of the role seriously.

Because of the technical nature of Tyrone's qualifications, my associate with an IT background took an additional session and then joined me for the mock interviews at the end. By bringing in an unfamiliar person for mock interviews, the candidate is placed in a situation closer to the upcoming interview.

Beverley's experience

"Interviewing for a first job can be a daunting process, but actually getting an interview is even harder to do. Degrees, Diplomas and High School Certificates are an essential part of the process of becoming a member of employed and financially independent adult society. It is difficult to place a value on those years of effort in acquiring a useful and in-demand skillset if one remains unemployed after graduating. Doing well in a course and building the said skillset does not build one's self-esteem and give one confidence if they are not getting one past the start line in the recruitment process.

BESPOKEN offered Tyrone the opportunity to open those doors in the recruitment process by coaching and thoroughly preparing him for it. The course was thorough and individualised and based on the first interview and assessment, where goals and concerns are discussed, strengths and weaknesses established.

He was then guided through the recruitment process, beginning with a general strategy, CV preparation and evaluation, interview processes and styles, and effective communication, from written to spoken format. Our son, a GIS (Geographic Information Systems) honours graduate had been actively looking for work for four months, without much success.

Within two weeks, he was getting numerous responses after submitting his CV, had a number of interviews with prospective employers and was offered two positions. He is now gainfully employed and confidently interacting with his bosses and peers. The skills gained as a result of the coaching will continue to be useful throughout his career."

Tyrone's experience

"Having graduated with Honours in GIS and then travelling, I returned to South Africa expecting to find a job relatively easily. The reality was entirely different – I struggled for four months before approaching BESPOKEN for coaching.

Starting right at the basics, Fiona worked with me to construct a CV which, when completed, immediately started generating interest from companies. From there, we moved on to interview preparation – starting with how to conduct effective research into prospective companies which puts one on the front foot going into an interview. After this, we tackled the interview process itself – from questions and answers, to diction and positive body language.

Next, Fiona and her associate conducted several mock interviews with me and reviewed the positives and negatives of my performance in each one. Additionally, prior to each real interview I attended, we would conduct a mock interview as if I were interviewing with that company. As part of the entire coaching process, Fiona taught me a routine which included physical, vocal and presence exercises which helped me to centre myself and feel relaxed before beginning an interview. This process meant that, before I even spoke, I was already projecting the right attitude toward the interviewers.

At the end of the process, I had offers from several companies and was able to negotiate a highly competitive starting salary, which BESPOKEN also supported. The skills that I learned through BESPOKEN are not isolated to the process of searching for a job; in my current role, they are invaluable to interfacing with clients and peers within my company. I really valued the coaching I received: I went from struggling to get interviews to getting a jumpstart to my career."

Epilogue

So, there you have it – everything I can share with you about spoken communication over 22 years and more. I started this book to capture the knowledge that has been passed down to me from people who are mostly now gone. Their legacy is in me and others they have taught and inspired. I hope it's going to help you on your journey towards audience engagement. I trust that it will. I've thoroughly enjoyed the 18 months I've spent writing and editing this book.

In closing, I would like to remind you of the overall intention of *Breathtaking Communication*, and indeed my work: to help you realise your full potential. Oscar Wilde once said, 'Youth is wasted on the young' and I wonder if he wasn't referring to not just the beauty and enthusiasm of youth, but the insecurity that stops us from being our complete selves when we are younger. Perhaps it's impossible because we don't quite know what it means to be ourselves as we are busy discovering who that self really is. But part of that discovery has got to be the process of speaking up and speaking out, because in doing so we find out just how large our lives can be as we hear the echoes reverberate back to us.

I am also reminded of the beautiful words penned by Marianne Williamson:

Epilogue

"Our deepest fear is not that we are inadequate. Our deepest fear is that we are powerful beyond measure. It is our light not our darkness that most frightens us. We ask ourselves, who am I to be brilliant, gorgeous, talented and fabulous? Actually, who are you not to be?"[1]

I hope you are encouraged to be your authentic self as you take up and embed the tools and techniques I've provided. But also remember that you are most often called to speak in your role as a subject matter expert or leader. Wear that role like an ermine robe and let it give you confidence as you speak.[2]

So, speak up, speak out, take chances. Get it wrong, get it right, learn and have fun doing so. Ask questions, grasp opportunities and smile. What's the worst that can happen to you, or anyone around you? No one is going to die as a result of you making a mistake! Be kind and be generous and recommend this book if you think it will help anyone else.

Appendices

Appendix 1
Some Additional Exercises

If you struggle with any aspect of preparing to speak, you might find it helpful to add additional exercises from here to enhance your daily or weekly routine.

Five exercises to help you focus

Let's face it; it's not always easy to focus. As soon as we attempt to clear our minds, thoughts start rushing in. It can be like holding the tide back with one hand! Sometimes, it's easy. These are for the harder times. Whether you're about to speak, in the early stages of planning, or practising the material you've put together, I hope you find them helpful.

These exercises will help with relaxation, breathing and focus. They're based on my morning quiet times, what some might call meditation, practise in my teaching and coaching work, and occasionally, when there's been a long gap in the day between my Rondo Sequence and my speech delivery, I will draw on one of these while I am waiting to speak. Dip in and out of them as the need arises. They should take anywhere from three to ten minutes, depending on which one you choose.

For each one, start by finding a position that's comfortable for you. Close your eyes or find a fixed point in front of you above eye level. I always close my eyes unless I think I'm in danger of falling asleep! Some of these exercises can double up as sleeping aids but decide what your desired outcome is before you start. Energetic speaking, or being quietly and calmly present in a meeting; they require different energy. If you're going to speak professionally, don't do the lying down exercises beforehand.

Most of them require visualisation. I have refrained from repeating the word 'imagine', but I hope you can.

1. A simple breathing exercise

Become aware of your breathing. As you breathe in, become aware of your lung capacity as your rib cage expands and your diaphragm flattens. As you breathe out, become aware of your body's ability to expel the air as your rib cage contracts and your diaphragm lifts. On a subsequent breath, become aware of how you can increase your lung capacity just by focusing on it. Now suspend your breath for a few seconds before exhaling, becoming aware of the stillness of your body before exhaling. Repeat for as long as you need or as time allows. I've deliberately not suggested counting at any stage as it's a good idea to simply tune into your body and breathing as you experience this exercise.

2. A two-minute breathing exercise for focus and relaxation

In this exercise, I suggest taking at least three breaths for each part. This is also great if you're struggling to sleep!

- Eyes closed often works best. Listen outside the room to all the sounds you can hear as you breathe deeply. Keep listening keenly until you've identified the furthest away sound, the highest sound, the lowest sound, the loudest, the softest sound, its frequency, whether it's natural or human made and anything else you notice. Tune in.

- Now draw your attention inside the room. What can you hear? Repeat as above. Take your time.
- Finally, draw your attention to the sound or rhythm of your body. Become intensely aware of it. This is often just your breath or your heartbeat. Really focus on it.
- Bring your focus back to your body in the room. Breathe. Then place the room in the house and the house in the community. Breathe. Open your eyes when you're ready. Experience the peace and focus.

3. Body check exercise

This is best done lying down. If you want to do it before speaking, sit in a chair and imagine you are lying down. Do it slowly, each phrase on a breath.

- Imagine you are on the shore of a beautiful, sandy beach. As you lie and relax, you can experience the sun shining on you. You can't see it but it's very real. Breathe in and out slowly and deeply, in rhythm with the sea as the tide comes in and flows out.
- As you breathe in, imagine the tide coming in and touching your feet. Tense them by curling your toes as you breathe in, then relax and release the tension as you breathe out and the tide flows out.
- Now the tide flows in and reaches your calves. Pull your toes towards your knees and feel the stretch. Tense, then release as you breathe out.
- Next, the water reaches your thighs – tense breathing in, relax as you breathe out. You feel completely safe and know that you can trust this water.
- Slow and lengthening your breaths, imagine the tide coming in slowly – it reaches your buttocks. Tense, pinching them, breathing in and then out and relaxing.
- Continue with the water flowing to your lower back, pull in your abdomen as if you want your bellybutton to touch your spine. Tense as you inhale, relax as you exhale.

- Next, you become aware of the water reaching your hands. As you inhale make tight fists with your hands, releasing as the tide goes out and they relax, and your hands melt into the sand.
- Repeat with your lower and then upper arms, tensing then relaxing as you inhale and exhale.
- Now, notice the water reaching your upper back, arch it and tense as you inhale and exhale, then shoulders, pulling them towards your ears, then your neck … tense and relax, breathing in and then out.
- As the water reaches the back of your head, scrunch up your facial muscles as you inhale, relax as you exhale.
- You are now being carried, held by the tide.
- You are being held. Breathe in and breathe out as you hear the tide, in, out. Repeat until you are ready for the tide to go out and imagine the weight of your body making an impression as it rests in the sand.

If you're lying down, slowly, roll on to your side, then curl up your knees. Roll on to your hands and knees and bring yourself slowly up, like a cat (or the cat curl position in yoga if you're familiar with that). Keeping your head relaxed, sit back onto your heels and open your eyes. Stand up carefully and slowly. Those with low blood pressure can feel lightheaded if you stand too quickly, but this deep breathing can also lead to light headedness. If you're seated, bring your attention back into the room and open your eyes.

4. Magic carpet ride breathing and relaxation exercise

This is best done lying down. You need to start by imagining you're lying on a magic carpet that will allow you to fly safely and travel through solid objects. If you are a highly visual learner, you may wish to visualise the colours and pattern of the carpet.

You are going to go to a place that you want to be, a place of peace, a place of quiet. It may be a green pasture, a mountain top, or a beach.

Decide on your destination. Take slow, deep breaths. As you breathe in, you rise up, as you breathe out you move forward. Slowly, imagine you are rising up from the room you are in and moving out of the window, being carried on a magic carpet. As you breathe in, the carpet rises up; as you breathe out, it moves forward. You feel completely safe.

As you leave your home, you visualise it from overhead. Again, as you rise above your neighbourhood, then your community. You are rising upwards and away, and everything is getting smaller – your region, province, country.

You are now rising above the clouds. There is peace and quiet. Take as long as you like, as many breaths as you wish, travelling to your imagined destination. Imagine the clouds. Respond to what you see.

When you are ready, you will begin to descend. Now your ingoing breath brings you down through the clouds and your outgoing breath continues to bring you forward, or down as needs be. The carpet knows perfectly how to take you to where you need to be. Trust and relax into it.

You arrive. Continue to breathe deeply. I always imagine I am unseen. Imagine the sounds around you. What would you hear in this imagined place?

Now focus on the smells … what would you smell? Take your time to imagine each one.

Next, what would you feel? Are there textures you can imagine at your fingertips, or through your skin? What is the temperature? Is it wet or dry? Can you imagine a breeze on your skin?

What would you imagine tasting?

Finally, imagine what you would see if you opened your eyes.

You can also do this exercise for the return journey and just reverse the ascent from your destination and travel home until you are back in your room.

5. Relaxation and breathing exercise: Melting wax

This can be done in any position but do get comfortable. I will talk you through it as if you are kneeling in an upright position.

Imagine you are made of wax. Breathe deeply. The sun is shining hot and bright. You enjoy its heat and light. Slowly, it transforms you from something hard and cold into something warm and malleable, until you become liquid.

You feel the sun warm on your face and your features slowly soften. Then your head and neck – breathe and let your head slowly drop on to your chest. The heat is on your arms, down into your fingers. Breathe deeply and slowly as you find them becoming soft and warm. Next, your chest: you can feel your internal organs becoming soft and malleable and the sun shines on them and breathing becomes easier and deeper, right into your abdomen where the heat of the sun has now reached.

The heat spreads into your buttocks and you slowly drop back onto your ankles (if you haven't done so already) and feel the heat soften your thighs and then your calves. Depending on your flexibility, you may wish to slowly 'melt' forwards so that your head is on your knees, or you may wish to melt slowly into a curled, foetal position on the floor. You may wish to go from one to the other. Either way, the final position is either lying on your stomach or back imagining you are a warm pool of wax, completely relaxed and translucent.

Appendix 1

Five vocal exercises

Here is a selection of additional vocal exercises I've used over the years for clients who struggle with articulation or accent. I've also used them with clients who come to me when Speech Therapy provision has been exhausted or not yet provided.

1. Vocal warm-ups

The context for these is after Step 14 'Mmmm-aaaah' in the Rondo Sequence in Chapter 9.

Ooooh-aaaah

Aaee-aaah

Eeeeeh-aaah

Iiieee-aaah

Oooo-aaah

Uuuuh-aaah

Ooooh-aaah

2. Working speech muscles

For Facial agility:

- Strong – b, d, l, ng (e.g., bad dog lying down)
- That's vicious, many men, red lorry, yellow lorry

For emphasising the end of words:

- Hard, dove, brick, shawl, knot, earth

3. An all-in-one exercise

Shake your hands as though flicking something off them. Then your whole arms. Shake a foot, then a leg. Repeat with the other leg. Then shake your whole body as much as is comfortable, as a dog would do after climbing out of a river!

Stretch, whole body, either by reaching as high over your head as possible or having a whole body stretch and yawn.

Centre, using the Bespoken Technique of Posture.

End with gentle Ooo-ahh. Smile.

4. The 'Ha' exercise: For building breath support, fitness and Strength

Firstly, ensure you've done your Rondo Sequence, up to and including Step 12, to have the correct vocal support and connection.

> *"If you can control 'ha' you can control any sound"*
> Patsy Rodenburg

This isn't a replacement for steps 13 and 14 but can replace 15 and 16 occasionally. Always stop when you feel the support go.

- Try holding a chair or a heavy object over your head when releasing 'ha'– you can also do this with 's' and 'z'.
- Try to keep the sound steady and constant.
- Try it walking around and try it with different notes and different volumes.
- Release 'ha' going from standing to sitting on the floor, keeping it constant.

5. The gumboot exercise

This exercise combines stretching with jaw and tongue work and a little bit of breath and vocal work. So, if you want to capture some aspects of the Rondo Sequence in a short space of time before your speaking opportunity, this one is good fun, if somewhat disgusting to imagine.

- Begin with the Chewing Gum Exercises from Step 12 of the Rondo Sequence.
- Imagine spitting the gum on the toe of one shoe.
- Stretch your feet at least shoulders' width apart and stretch your opposite hand high in the air
- Stretch down and imagine pulling the gum off your shoe, leaving some behind so there's a long string of gum as you stretch your arm back up in the air.
- Repeat, but this time, imagine successfully removing it from your shoe.
- Pop the imagined gum back in your mouth and repeat, this time spitting it onto the other foot.
- At the end, imagine spitting the gum onto the floor in front of you with a strong, 'Ppaa'.

Appendix 2
Elevator Pitch Worksheet

Networking: Introducing yourself and your business

Having a one to two-minute Elevator Pitch is a great opportunity at networking events to not only promote yourself and your work, but it's essential for informing your fellow networkers about what it is you are looking for.

The key to successful networking often lies in successful communication about your business along with the ability to show and inspire others to help you grow your business through referrals.

Getting it right is not an exact science and it will change somewhat every time. I recommend consistently reflecting on your performance and practising every time. Adapt it accordingly for a one-to-one introduction or speaking to a room full of people.

Before you begin, you might want to ask yourself the following questions:

What is a current barrier to my effective networking?
What will success look like?
How much does this mean to me? What is the value of this?

Preparation

Practise what you want to say in the car, or as you walk to the event, preferably aloud (if walking, practise at home!). What do you want people to know today about you and your business? This will mean that you are calmer and more confident when you speak.

What do you want people to remember about you/your business the next day?

Is there something you can say that's attention grabbing? How can you make it memorable? What was memorable about the last good one you heard? Consider using a prop if it helps.

Use a note if you have to (but try not to), until you feel confident without having it written down. Don't worry, if it's not your job to present, people will be compassionate. If you use a note, ensure it is in bullet point format and large print – not caps as it's difficult to read.

Keep your finger on the line you're reading and try to look up and make eye contact occasionally. Smile, and find other friendly faces in the room.

Do try to move away from it soon – just speak from the heart about your work and keep it short – it will be fine!

An Elevator Pitch Is 60-120 seconds!

To give you an idea, that's about 120-240 written words. Try not to go over. It's inconsiderate and some people will switch off because they're put off! Then you have lost them.

Roughly, your name, company and profession take about ten seconds, you could take 30 seconds for talking about one area of your business, ten seconds to say what you're looking for at the moment and what we can do, then repeat your name and company again. Keep it simple. Be specific.

Outline for Elevator Pitch

Introduction (*10-15 Seconds*)

Name, Business/Organisation Name:

Middle (*30-60 Seconds*)

Overview of products/services and what you require:

Call To Action (*10-20 Seconds*)

Location/where you are looking for business; how your audience can help:

Conclusion (*10-15 Seconds*)

Your name, your organisation's name and/or profession, possibly your strapline.

Appendix 3
A Special for Faith Leaders and Communities

In my introduction, you will have read that I was raised as a churchgoer – every Sunday like clockwork. This was the cultural norm growing up in Ireland in the '70s and '80s. Since then, I've sought to experience a variety of worship, faith and religion. All of them require effective communication skills, be it speaking or listening. Individuals within faith groups vary widely in their ability to do this well or badly. As someone who found a personal faith in their twenties following several years of searching, I have a special interest in helping faith leaders to engage effectively with their audiences,[1] congregations, and worshippers in a way that is sincere and honours the deity in which they profess a faith.

No one has ever been endeared to a platform through boredom or disconnection. In fact, that is why often, many are driven away. It is my hope that with my fairly unique combination of voice and speech coaching, Time to Think methodology and my personal faith, I may be able to offer some ideas to start a conversation about this in your place of worship.

Full disclosure: Despite being very interested in doing so, I've not been to a synagogue, mosque or temple, or experienced their services in person, sometimes because I haven't been invited, or the invitation hasn't been followed through. My experience is limited to a wide variety of Christian denominations in several countries and languages. But I wish to in no way limit the possibility that the information I'm providing is applicable across a variety of religions.

How effectively do we communicate in our holy places – to each other and to visitors? What if we had a mystery shopper litmus test? Sadly, there is one story I became aware of some years ago that gave me pause for thought.

In his autobiography,[2] Mahatma Gandhi wrote that while he was studying, he read the Gospels and considered the Christian faith. One Sunday, he attended a local church with the intention of speaking to the minister. But when he arrived, the usher apparently refused to give him a seat and suggested he go and worship with his own people. He said he left the church and decided, "If Christians have a caste system, I might as well remain a Hindu."

My hope is that those who wish to welcome new people to their places of worship will communicate the right message with what they say and do with their speech, writing, body and words. If I apply my expertise to faith settings, there are several ingredients to consider. Where this ingredient is discussed in more detail, I will refer to that chapter in parentheses.

Place – environment and personal (See Chapter 18)

Does the building in which you meet say 'you matter' to the audience? Is it welcoming and will a first-time visitor know where to go and what is expected of them? Insecurity around fear of getting it wrong can be a barrier to people. Are the notices informative, polite and friendly? All capitals writing is seen by most people as shouting; rather make notices written in lower case and just make the font larger.

Seating is also important to consider. I recommend reminding the audience from time to time that regular attendance doesn't mean they have a confirmed seat. It would be ridiculous to anticipate this anywhere except a theatre or cinema where you book a seat, so why do people in organised religious groups get this wrong? As the saying goes, familiarity breeds contempt and if your familiarity with your place of worship breeds contempt in you for visitors, don't expect your group to grow or gain a positive reputation in the community.

In terms of embodying Place in how we show up, do visitors and attendees know what is expected in terms of their appearance? Tourists visiting holy places on holidays usually look on a website to see how to dress appropriately, e.g., certain parts of their bodies must be covered, and certain footwear is recommended. Does your website reflect this so that your local community know that they can just arrive as they are, or not? Generally, when we go to a new place, we wonder what the dress code is. Why should we expect first-time visitors to know when visiting our places of worship? If the message you send out is 'All Welcome Here' you had better show up in a way that shows you mean it!

Position and positions

Are there barriers between you and your audience, such as distance or access?

Communicate all this information on your website. Is there an annual audit to ensure that a visitor could easily find their way to your place of worship and once they arrive, is visitor parking clearly marked or information about parking available elsewhere?

At least one Greeter or Welcomer should be on duty by the entrance. Their priority is to ensure visitors are warmly welcomed and feel comfortable in your setting. Empathy is the number one requirement. What would you want to know if you entered a strange new place surrounded by people who seem to know each other and what is going on? A welcome leaflet to browse later can be helpful, as one doesn't usually absorb everything first time around, and this information should be updated along with the website on a regular basis.

Respecting people's time (see Chapter 2)

Even amongst faithful adherents, this can be an issue. Whilst a time of worship should be a sacrifice of praise and not a clock-watching experience, respect needs to come from both sides. Managing expectations through effective communication will ensure that people experience psychological safety during their time at your place of worship. I have sometimes thought that the leader or preacher has been too spoilt for too long by a captive and polite audience and may unwittingly take advantage of this.

There are cultural considerations to take on board too. Anyone attending a proper African service, for instance, needs to put their watch to one side, or leave it at home, and simply enter the experience. Communication is often a whole-body experience, and the volume may be louder and more passionate than that to which most Europeans are accustomed. By contrast, hourly Sunday services in a largely Roman Catholic country means that the service is usually over in 40-45 minutes, in order to allow for people to leave and the organisers to prepare for the next service. Where appropriate, websites can communicate these expectations to adherents and would-be visitors alike.

Many of the aspects of a service are repeated across a month or in an annual cycle and this influences timings. One such aspect repeated weekly is the sermon, homily or message in a Christian service. What is the right length for this message, which is based on a Bible passage or passages and prepared by the preacher or leader for that week? This is very much a 'how long is a piece of string' type question and it would be wrong of me to say that there is a right answer. What I would suggest is that 21st century audiences have become used to short, succinct messages, or soundbites. While I don't agree that modern audiences have a shorter attention span, I do believe it is more challenging to engage our attention for a longer time period as the pace of life has increased and social media engages us with soundbites.

The popularity of TED talks has made 18 minutes the ideal length of time for engaging an audience. Research has shown[3] that humans can comfortably focus for about 20 minutes before our mind wanders. Therefore, 18-20 minutes is a reasonable limit to expect a seated audience to engage. This would suggest that a speaker is faced with a decision: to either do the necessary work to engage and sustain an audience's attention for longer with additional tools and techniques of modulation, content and visual aids, or to restrict their talk to engage their audience for 18-20 minutes. This is not to diminish your ability to speak for longer or indeed the ability of a higher power to engage the audience. But I would challenge a faith leader to ask themselves these questions: Is it possible to say what I feel led to say in 20 minutes, and am I prepared to put the work in to be concise enough to do so? If you are going to speak for longer, are you prepared to lose some of the congregation as their attention wavers? The holy books are filled with stories of leaders who got messages across succinctly to their audiences and the Sermon on the Mount and their equivalent seem to be the exception rather than the rule.

Language

Do your audience understand the language used? Is there unhelpful, outdated jargon that could isolate them? Leaders should do a sense check of content for every service from the perspective of an outsider. What do you need to explain? Strive to get the balance right; the regular audience don't want to hear the same explanations every week. If very little needs explaining, that makes life less complicated. Could you put a page on your website to explain language that is special to your faith group?

Smile (See Chapter 6)

In the effort to be serious, a smile is often forgotten. I believe the two should never be mutually exclusive. Remember, a smile says, 'I'm happy you're here' or 'You are welcome'. A quote incorrectly attributed to Maya Angelou expands beautifully, "I've learned that people will forget what you said, people will forget what you did, but people will never forget how you made them feel."[4] Effective communication can do this, and a smile is an essential ingredient in most settings.

I've also noticed that many of us don't seem to have the words in mind when singing joyful songs, based on the expression on many faces I see! Is our face expressing what we're saying and singing?

Appendix 3

Reading Aloud (Chapter 10 and 20)

How much of your gathering is reading based? Is this inclusive of people with learning difficulties? Spoken word or words that are read aloud will make it easier for those with dyslexia or visual and learning difficulties to engage, and know that light writing on a plain, dark background is easier to read. It's worth noting that if collective singing is included or expected, the words being sung are a reading requirement for your audience. What considerations do you need to make for this?

For reasons explained in Chapter 10, whoever reads should practise aloud a few times to ensure the text flows for listeners and difficult words and names are mastered in advance.

Are the texts read in a way that brings the text to life? Are the characters represented in a way that demonstrates their character accurately? As an adult, I realised that I had subconsciously imagined Mary, mother of Jesus to be quite a weak person. Through my studies toward speech and drama teaching, I realised that because all the leaders in my church were men where I grew up, they had lightened and weakened their voices to characterise Mary's female voice. She became a far more relatable and exciting figure when I realised this. I can highly recommend David Suchet's reading of the UKNIV Bible, for an exquisite rendition of this library of books.[5] On the subject of holy book translations, it's worth finding a translation that gets the balance right between accuracy and modern English. Those that are too devoted to accurate translation can be clumsy to read and those that don't strive for accuracy are perhaps not ideal reading in a service and more suitable for private reading.

Modulation (Chapter 11)

Are you varying your voice to engage and interest your audience? I only know of one church service that lasted 20 minutes or less,[6] but even that much listening requires changes in our vocal variety. This applies to both speaking and reading. There was a time when preachers had to speak slowly and carefully because of how sound travelled in cavernous stone buildings, and this affected their ability to use modulation effectively. However, there is no excuse for this today. It's remarkable how common it is for religious leaders to believe they must use a different voice for their audiences when they are in the pulpit, and it's not limited by age, unfortunately. Some years ago, a woman introduced me to her son in South Africa and he sounded just like you or me. However, that Sunday he preached in the service and his voice was almost unrecognisable. I was confounded and it took all my strength to restrain from rushing up to him afterwards and preaching the good news that he could speak like a human! Hallelujah, we now have microphones and (mostly) acoustically sympathetic buildings. We can now speak authentically from the heart, or gut as you will have learned by now.

It seems appropriate to end this Appendix with a verse that encompasses Islam, Judaism and Christianity and speaks of talking about the writings of the holy books:

'Hear, O Israel: the Lord our God, the Lord is one. Love the Lord your God with all your heart and with all your soul and with all your strength. These commandments that I give you today are to be on your hearts. Impress them on your children. *Talk about them when you sit at home and when you walk along the road, when you lie down and when you get up.'*[7] (my emphasis)

Appendix 4
Rondo Sequence

1. **Spine:** Stretch up, breathe deeply, relax, exhale three times.
2. **Head/neck:** roll three times, shoulder to shoulder.
3. **Shoulder:** roll, separately three times. Roll or lift and drop together three times.
4. **Arms**: Lunge and rotate three times one way, then then other.
5. **Posture**: Align, unlock, lift, rock. Eyes, breathe deeply, exhale on count of ten.

(SUPPORT)

6. **Chest:** Open arms wide and palms forward. Two breaths, then count to ten.
7. **Sides**: Legs apart, stretch arms alternately overhead.
8. **Back:** Hug and drop forwards, head hanging loosely.

   Breathe, drop arms. Breathe. Rise slowly on one to 16 on third exhale.

(OPEN)

9. **Diaphragm:** With a partner or wall/door. Exhale on ten.
10. **Kabuki** – Posture with knees bent, breathe to emotional centre for ten.
11. **Throw ball** – Throw, think timing of release of breath, then 'throw' word.

(CONNECT)

12. **Jaw, tongue and soft palate exercises**

    - *Jaw:* Biting an apple.
    - *Tongue:* Licking an ice-cream (plus ears or NSEW).
    - *Tongue:* Brush teeth with tongue.
    - *Both:* Chewing gum (more and more) closed then open.
    - *Soft palate:* Yawn - open, then closed.
    - *Jaw and facial muscles:* Whole face massage.

(RELEASE)

13. **Resonance 1:** Hum into five resonators (mouth, nose, throat, chest, head).
14. **Resonance 2:** 'Mmm' (five) – 'aah' (wide as possible to fade).

(RESONATE)

15. **Vocal 1**: Breathe deeply, exhaling 'sss', then 'zzz' for a count of 15-35.
16. **Vocal 2**: Breathe to hand, elbow, arms-length, wall, corner, room.

    Repeat with 'Yes'.

(OUT)

Appendix 5
Seated Rondo Sequence

1. **Spine:** Reach, stretch, hold for 3. Exhale Repeat x 3.
2. **Head-neck roll:** Roll x 3.
3. **Shoulders:** Roll x 3, separately then together, or receive massage to ease tension.
4. **Arms:** Squeeze hands - inhale, release - exhale x 3
5. **Posture:** Seated posture, align. Raise sternum, exhale. Eyes, breathe deeply, exhale 10.

   Support

6. **Chest:** (PA) Open arms wide and palms forward. Exhale on ten.
7. **Sides:** Supported by sitting squarely in the chair, stretch arms alternately overhead.
8. **Back:** Hug yourself and drop forwards, head hanging loosely.

   Open

   Drop arms. Breathe. Rise slowly on one to about 16.

9. **Diaphragm:** (PA) Connection 1: Press hands against hands and push.

   Count aloud to ten on the outgoing breath.

   Connect

10. **Throw ball -** Connection 2: timing of release of breath – 'Yes!'

11. **Jaw/tongue exercises**

    - Biting an apple.
    - Licking an ice-cream (plus ears or NSEW).
    - Brush teeth with tongue.
    - Chew gum (more and more) closed then open.
    - Yawn closed then open.
    - Massage.

    Release

12. **Resonance 1:** Hum into all resonators – mouth, throat, chest, nose, head.
13. **Resonance 2:** Mmm-ah.

    Resonate

14. **Vocal 1**: Breathe deeply, exhaling 's', 'z' for count of 15, 20, 25, 30, 35.
15. **Vocal 2**: Breathe to hand, arms-length, wall, corner, room. Then 'Yes'.

    Out

Notes

Introduction

1. The Association of Irish Musical Societies.
2. Both programmes were produced and televised by the British Broadcasting Corporation (BBC)
3. I have experienced the benefits personally and this article talks about the proven results of talk therapy https://www.forbes.com/sites/alicegwalton/2017/01/25/research-again-finds-that-talk-therapy-can-change-the-brain/
4. Ted Talk, Amy Cuddy *Your Body Language Shapes Who You Are*, June 8th, 2013, accessed 10th April, 2017.
5. This is known as a high school in many other countries.
6. Time to Think by Nancy Kline, 1999, Ward Lock, Octopus Publishing Group, London

Glossary of Terms

1. These definitions have been collected over several years. Many are from notes given by teachers; others are based on dictionary definitions. A few are my own definitions.

Chapter 1

1. 8 "Doh-a-deer", Sound of Music, Rogers & Hammerstein (1965)
2. Based on the writings, teaching and practice of Nancy Kline at the Time to Think Foundation.
3. STEM is a collective term used to describe people in Science, Technology, Engineering and Maths-related industries.
4. Habit two from Stephen R. Covey's 1989 *7 Habits of Highly Effective People* Simon and Schuster,.

Chapter 2

1. This is an opportunity for people to share who they are and what they do in the time it would take to tell someone who asked in a lift or an elevator, before the doors open. Every sentence is impactful and delivers the most important information first.
2. This has been attributed to President Woodrow Wilson (1856-1924), but he was employing a saying that was in use at the time.

Chapter 3

1. John F. Kennedy, Address to Joint Session of Congress, on Urgent National Needs, Release No: 60-83F (25 May 1961).
2. www.Vark-learn.com
3. Oxford Languages dictionary https://languages.oup.com/google-dictionary-en/
4. Felder, R.M. and Brent, R., 2003. Random Thoughts: Learning by Doing. *Chemical Engineering Education*, 37(4), pp.282-283.

Chapter 4

1. https://www.jvoice.org/article/S0892-1997(16)00008-4/fulltext   accessed   10th January 2022
2. Tapping a finger or jiggling a knee are two common ones.
3. I heard this first from Patsy Rodenburg in a workshop. She speaks about it in her book *Power Presentation*, Penguin Books, 2009.
4. Full credit to Mannie Babington-Smith, an Austrian physiotherapist I attended in Didcot in the '00s. She gave me this as an exercise when I had a gardening injury and I added it to my sequence of exercises for my student and clients immediately.

Chapter 5

1. https://www.healthline.com/nutrition/gut-brain-connection#TOC_TITLE_HDR_2, accessed 7th October 2021
2. https://www.wimhofmethod.com/vagus-nerve-stimulation#:~:text=Deep%20breathing.,neurons%20that%20detect%20blood%20pressure, accessed 7th October 2021

Chapter 6

1. https://www.sclhealth.org/blog/2019/06/the-real-health-benefits-of-smiling-and-laughing/ accessed 10th May 2022

Chapter 7

1. https://www.merriam-webster.com/dictionary/resonance
2. Credit for this latter idea goes to my dear musician friend, Philippa Spits.
3. Patsy Rodenburg, Workshop quote from 2000, Johannesburg, South Africa.

Chapter 8

1. Patsy Rodenburg shared that seven repeats of 35 seconds is a normal expectation for her students and her clients, but stage work is extremely demanding day in day out, so decide what's appropriate and helpful for you.

Chapter 9

1. Dino Music, DNCD 1222, CD, Netherland, 1989

Chapter 10

1. Shared by Joan Lee, LTCL, of Joan Lee Theatre Arts School, Johannesburg, my Speech and Drama Coach in South Africa between 1998-2002.
2. I do have a client for which reading aloud was a huge barrier. Confronting and removing that barrier was a major step in her giving herself permission to take her public speaking to the next level. This has only happened once in 21 years, but if that's you too, do whatever you need in order to take that next step.
3. 'Education, Literacy and the Reading Public', Amy J. Lloyd, University of Cambridge, Gale Primary Sources, accessed online 8th August, 2022, p.2.

Chapter 11

1. Oxford English Dictionary
2. *Sounds like a winner: voice pitch influences perception of leadership capacity in both men and women*, 2012, https://www.ncbi.nlm.nih.gov/pmc/articles/PMC3350713/; *Why We Prefer Masculine Voices (Even in Women)*, 2012, The Atlantic https://www.theatlantic.com/sexes/archive/2012/12/why-we-prefer-masculine-voices-even-in-women/266350/;
3. *Lord of the Flies* by William Golding, Faber and Faber, 1954
4. Most mobile phones have recording apps. Please understand that the quality of the recording won't reflect your true voice as it's just a sample of the sound. Try not to be self-critical.
5. Joan Lee was quoting someone called Maisie. I didn't catch her surname at the time which is a shame as I've had cause to quote it often since.
6. Published by Penguin, 2003.
7. I have been unable to recall the title of this book.
8. I grew up in the home of a racecourse, Clonmel, and nearby famous racing stables, but my parents were in possession of three betting shops and a pub where racing was transmitted most Saturdays.

Chapter 12

1. The Merchant of Venice, Act IV, Scene I, William Shakespeare, 1596.
2. A word of acknowledgement: I know this may seem quite weird and foreign as exercises go. You just need to decide to do it anyway and enjoy the benefits. Anecdotally, I was doing this with a client once and a big, black tomcat was passing through the garden on the way to the orchard behind. He got such a fright with the sounds coming from us, that he froze and went up on all his claws as if we were a threat! My client, a very serious chap, who had been struggling with smiling and tended to grimace instead, laughed uproariously at the expression on the cat's face.

Chapter 13

1. In case like me, you love a complicated word, consonants are divided into groups based on which organs of speech we use to form them. For example, b is a bi-labial plosive because we use both lips to form the sound. You get voiced and unvoiced consonants, where voiced originate in the voice box and unvoiced are created with interrupted airflow in the mouth. Z and S are examples of each.

Chapter 14

1. Devoicing is when our voice sits in our throat, and we lack vocal power as a result.
2. Another meaning of this acronym is Keep It Simple Stupid, but I'm not fond of this one!

Chapter 15

1. TED is a non-profit organisation founded in 1984, devoted to spreading ideas, usually in the form of short, powerful talks of 18 minutes or less. Originally a conference where Technology, Entertainment and Design converged, today talks covers almost all topics in more than 100 languages.
2. You may disagree with this because you are a person that speeds up when you're nervous. This will no longer be happening if you've embedded The Rondo Sequence from Section Two and pace from Chapter 11.
3. https://www.youtube.com/watch?v=0SUTInEaQ3Q, Nervous vs. Excitement by Simon Sinek, YouTube, 16 May 2018, accessed 12th June 2018 and many times since then to share with clients.
4. Not their real names.
5. Acknowledgement for these three questions on feedback go to Jason Lane of Innovista who shared them at a talk, *What is the most neglected aspect of Leadership Development?* In Oxford, 12th December, 2019.
6. From the book *The Devil to Pay* by Jack Youngblood and Robin Moore, Page 218, Coward McCann, Inc., New York. The quote is popularly attributed to Gary Player, amongst other golfers but refers to shooting in the book.

Chapter 16

1. Lighting and sound equipment is dealt with in detail by those more interested in technical aspects of it, and some are sponsored by equipment providers. My aim is to focus on what you need to do to improve audience experience and you can decide what to invest, using subject matter experts to recommend the best equipment. I would recommend Frank Furness (frankfurness.com/) for such advice as he will only recommend equipment he trusts and uses himself.
2. RODE SmartLav+ is a decent affordable mic with an extension cable which ensures your movement isn't too limited. The features that mattered to me were sound quality and price with a good rating, so an equivalent with similar features would be just as good, if that's what matters to you.

3. Modulation is covered in Chapter 11.

Chapter 18

1. This and all subsequent quotations in this chapter are from *Time to Think* by Nancy Kline or spoken by her during her course delivery.
2. Details of all books and courses are available at www.timetothink.com
3. The quotations are from Kline's latest book *The Promise That Changes Everything – I Won't Interrupt You*, Nancy Kline, Penguin Random House UK, 2020.
4. 2003, Are You Following Jesus Or Just Fooling Around?! by Dr. Ray Cummings, Quote Page 81, Xulon Press: Salem Media Group, Camarillo, California. Brown uses the quotation in her Audible book, The Gifts of Imperfection, (APA. Brown, B. (2010). Gifts of imperfection, the: Hazelden Information & Educational Services.)
5. Sinek, S., 2011. *Start with why: How great leaders inspire everyone to take action*, London: Penguin Books Ltd.
6. Studies which provide evidence for this area are popular in research for child development and old age; it would be logical to assume that it matters throughout life. https://www.ncbi.nlm.nih.gov/pmc/articles/PMC2654994/
7. Maslow, A. H. (1943). A Theory of Human Motivation. *Psychological Review, 50*(4), 370–396,"

Chapter 19

1. Not his real name. All names have been changed to protect client confidentiality.
2. https://www.ted.com/talks/alanna_shaikh_coronavirus_is_our_future? language=en, accessed 28th March 2020.
3. Julia Gillard's misogyny speech, Channer 10, https://www.youtube.com/watch?v= SOPsxpMzYw4, first viewed on 12th August 2022.
4. Tony Buzan, The Mindmap Book, Pearson, 2010.
5. Toastmasters International is a non-profit peer-mentoring organisation that helps develop public speaking and leadership skills through a worldwide network of clubs.

Chapter 20

1. Madelaine Black, *Why I'm Shaming Shame*, TEDx Talks, 16th March 2022 https://www.youtube.com/watch?v=rqXluB4l1c8, accessed 10th April, 2022
2. Abhinaya Darpanam is a Sanskrit treatise on Indian classical dances, having a detailed account of dance movements and expressions. https://narthaki.-com/info/articles/art484.html **'Abhinaya Darpanam' in a nutshell,** Dr. Maithili Nesargi-Naik, May 14, 2020 Accessed 25th May, 2020
3. 'How to Avoid Death by PowerPoint' by David Phillips, speaker, author and coach in modern presentation skills, TEDx Stockholm https://www.youtube.com/watch?v=Iwpi1Lm6dFo&t=23s, first accessed 14th October 2018.
4. Murre JMJ, Dros J (2015) Replication and Analysis of Ebbinghaus' Forgetting Curve. PLoS ONE 10(7): e0120644. https://doi.org/10.1371/journal.pone.0120644 website accessed 14th October 2018.

5. Source: https://www.dyslexia-reading-well.com/dyslexia-statistics.html website accessed 14th October 2018.

Chapter 21

1. Retrospective questions are popular in the Lean and Agile community, but the technique was inspired by Virginia Satir (1916-1988), the "mother of family therapy".
2. The Johari Window Model illustrates a team's dynamics, based on the trust between team members. The tool is used to gain a better understanding of how a leader and team members interact with each other.
3. The origin of the BOOST model is unknown. University of California, Irvine have the earliest use of it recorded online, that I can find.
4. Steven Moffat, BBC, Shelock (2014), Series 3, Episode 2, 'The Sign of Three', 8:30pm 5 Jan 2014
5. https://www.bbc.co.uk/iplayer/episode/b03ny7ng/sherlock-series-3-2-the-sign-of-three.
6. Benedict Cumberbatch has a degree in Drama from University of Manchester and an MA in Classic Acting from LAMDA.
7. This case study originally appeared as an article on BESPOKEN's website at https://bespoken.org.uk/coaching-sherlock/

Epilogue

1. *Return to Love* by Marianne Williamson, Harper Collins, 1992.
2. Mantle of the Expert is an approach I was introduced to when I was studying speech and drama teaching, but the words 'mantle of the expert' developed by Dorothy Heathcote inspired me to use this image to inspire others.

Appendix 3

1. I will refer to them as audiences as a generic term that transcends various faith groups.
2. M.K. Gandhi, An Autobiography: The Story of My Experiments with Truth, Penguin Classics, 2001.
3. Wilson TD, Reinhard DA, Westgate EC, Gilbert DT, Ellerbeck N, Hahn C, Brown CL, Shaked A. Social psychology. Just think: the challenges of the disengaged mind. Science. 2014 Jul 4;345(6192):75-7. doi: 10.1126/science.1250830. PMID: 24994650; PMCID: PMC4330241.
4. The core quote is "They may forget what you said - but they will never forget how you made them feel." ascribed to Carl W, Beuhner, 1971, Richard Evans' Quote Book by Richard L. Evans, ("Selected from the 'Spoken Word' and 'Thought for the Day' and from many inspiring thought-provoking sources from many centuries") Quote Page 244, Column 2, Publishers Press, Salt Lake City, Utah. (Verified with scans; thanks to the librarians of Harold B. Lee Library, Brigham Young University, Provo, Utah). I have quoted the version I find more eloquent.

5. Available at Bible Gateway, https://www.biblegateway.com/versions/New-International-Version-NIV-Bible/ and on YouTube at https://www.youtube.com/watch?v=jx_65lT1pUc&list=PLs0kYUO87ryQ58A2PZGnrHd4Ie1zFPzbn

6. When I was 24, I eloped with my now husband and the service was 20 minutes tops, but even that was punctuated with such variety as the exchange of rings and there were five different voices as we agreed to vows and had two witnesses.

7. This translation is taken from the Holy Bible, book of Deuteronomy, chapter six, verses 4-6.

Acknowledgements

There are so many people who have made this book possible, not just the physical copy you're holding in your hand or audio you're listening to. But it takes great courage to be vulnerable enough to commit our thinking, knowledge and experience to paper. This courage probably started back in South Africa when my husband, Andrew Scott, didn't laugh but believed I could become a Speech and Drama Teacher at 29 with a toddler. Thank you for your lifetime partnership and championing me as I created and birthed this book. I cannot thank but remember his late Mom, who was so proud of me as I progressed to opening my first studio and my last one too. I also had a committed group of local friends, particularly Raylene, Jane and Michelle who pledged their support and Philippa who was a constant laughing champion even as we flew away to the UK and has returned to my side since. Thank you. When I left the studios behind and became BESPOKEN, Cath and Jim Convery saw the successful trainer in me and Alistair Watkins my first mentor there. Thank you. I thank Marjory Mair, for the quality of her listening and questions, and for introducing me to Time to Think. Thank you, Nancy Kline, for unqualified permission to print what I wrote about Time to Think. This book would never have begun without Dr Charlotte Booth, my faithful book coach who encouraged me and boldly guided my right up to the fifth edit. Thank you, Luke, Georgia and Alex – the first, second and third child alongside this fourth child, for allowing me to be more than a mother, which is what I needed to be a mother. And for their insights in their areas of expertise when it came to images (Alex), typography (Georgia) and cover design (Luke and Georgia). Thanks to David Savage for coaching me past a publishing block and Frankie Walker for putting a face to publishing and introducing me to publishers who actually responded! Thank you, Patricia Sadler, my osteopath, who was available for ensuring a couple of exercises were safe for readers without my requirement to witness them being done. Thanks to Shelley Bridgman and Rikki Arundel of the PSA* for the conversations we had to maximise gender diversity and inclusion when referring to voice. Thanks to the *Professional Speaking Association, I have come to know and know of professionals who I could entrust this manuscript to for the Foreword and reviews – thank you Graeme Codrington, Lynda Shaw, Alan Stevens, Renee Lee Rosenburg (NSA, National Speakers Association, USA) and Patsy Rodenburg, voice and speech coach extraordinaire, for giving up their time and writing such kind words about my work. Thank you to The Alliance, my tribe in networking, for their ongoing encouragement and cheerleading, especially Kelly Drewett, for providing the creative space when I was battling with my final edit. Thanks to Lilly Liddicott and Camelle Daley – my Editor and Publisher respectively for being the midwives who delivered this baby! And thanks to the man who wrapped this baby up, Mark Wójcicki, Studio Stanley for such beautiful collaborative work on the book cover design. Thanks most of all to God, who created me with a purpose that is manifest in this book: to equip and empower people to communicate effectively. And for giving me parents who loved and fostered music, art and drama in their children and a father who raised me to believe I could be or do anything.

Printed in Great Britain
by Amazon